Homework
DONE RIGHT

This book is dedicated to our dear friend and coauthor,

Jere Brophy.

One week after our manuscript was sent to the editor, Jere Brophy passed away as the result of a massive heart attack. Jere was a dedicated husband, a proud father and grandfather, and a world-renowned educator. His unwavering commitment to excellence and his thoughtfulness inspired everyone who knew him. Jere was humble and kind, exhibited a dry sense of humor, expressed equity and equality in all his actions, and was truly brilliant! He was an amazing teacher, colleague, and friend.

Homework
DONE RIGHT

Powerful Learning in Real-Life Situations

Janet Alleman   **Barbara Knighton**   **Ben Botwinski**
Jere Brophy   **Rob Ley**   **Sarah Middlestead**

Skyhorse Publishing

Skyhorse Publishing books may be purchased in bulk at special discounts for sales promotion, corporate gifts, fund-raising, or educational purposes. Special editions can also be created to specifications. For details, contact the Special Sales Department, Skyhorse Publishing, 307 West 36th Street, 11th Floor, New York, NY 10018 or info@skyhorsepublishing.com.

Skyhorse® and Skyhorse Publishing® are registered trademarks of Skyhorse Publishing, Inc.®, a Delaware corporation.

Visit our website at www.skyhorsepublishing.com.

10 9 8 7 6 5 4 3 2 1

Library of Congress Cataloging-in-Publication Data is available on file.

Cover design by Michael Dubowe

Print ISBN: 978-1-62914-560-0
Ebook ISBN: 978-1-62914-991-2

Printed in China

Contents

Preface   vi

Acknowledgments   viii

About the Authors   x

PART I. REALIZE THE PURPOSE   1

1. What Is So Important About Homework?   2

2. What Is the Rationale for Homework?   8

3. What Do the Experts Say About Homework?   15

4. How Does Changing Homework Impact Your Practice?   26

PART II. ASSEMBLE THE PLAN   41

5. How Can You Design Meaningful Homework?   42

6. How Can You Put Meaningful Homework Into Action?   58

PART III. EXAMINE THE POSSIBILITIES   67

7. How Can Meaningful Homework Look
     in the Early Elementary Grades?   69

8. How Can Meaningful Homework Look
     in the Upper Elementary Grades?   80

9. How Can Meaningful Homework Look in Middle School?   93

10. How Can Meaningful Homework Look in High School?   104

11. Still Not Convinced?   116

Appendix A: Completed Homework Design Planning Form   127

Appendix B: Early Elementary Data Collection Tools   141

Appendix C: Upper Elementary Data Collection Tools   149

Appendix D: Middle School Data Collection Tools   161

Appendix E: High School Data Collection Tools   167

A Guide to Your Professional Learning   179

Index   199

Preface

This book is the product of over two years of extensive research, discussion, and reflection on the topic of homework by a team consisting of four public school educators, a university professor of teacher education, and a researcher on teaching. It describes the changes the teachers went through as they examined their own practices and pedagogy related to assignments for students outside the classroom. The book includes a brief description of the history of homework as well as an overview of current controversies and related research findings. Several examples are provided at each level (i.e., early elementary, upper elementary, middle school, and high school) of how good teaching can be supported and enhanced by meaningful homework.

Our team of teachers and researchers came together as the result of an action research conference at the Michigan State University College of Education in December 2007. Each of the four classroom teachers shared his or her personal journey in seeking more meaningful homework and the response of students and families. It became apparent early on that a set of common beliefs and strategies connected these authors and their experiences. Those beliefs and strategies are the foundation of this book.

Overall, these teachers have seen marked improvements in the attitude, attention, enthusiasm, and participation of students and their families. Each teacher could tell many stories of being approached by parents who were enthusiastic about an assignment and appreciative of the opportunity to make connections with their children. There are also many instances in which students have gone above and beyond what the homework projects called for, thus showing how motivating these assignments can be. These teachers, as well as others who are currently applying these ideas, work in a variety of K–12 settings ranging from rural, city, and suburban districts. This gives the authors confidence that you can replicate their results in your own practice, wherever you may teach. We recognize, too, that many teachers believe in the need to assign skills practice, and we encourage incorporating that practice into more meaningful assignments.

Although not written as a traditional text, this book should be useful as a resource in a variety of contexts. It would be valuable to support a group of teachers working together as a Professional Learning Community (PLC), as a yearlong school building improvement initiative, or as a study group for a specific subject area. The book could also serve as a text for a college or university course for preservice teachers. The "Guide to Your Professional Learning" at the end of the book supplies extra support to promote discussions and assist implementation of the ideas shared within the chapters.

TEXT ORGANIZATION

This book is divided into three sections: Part I: Realize the Purpose, Part II: Assemble the Plan, and Part III: Examine the Possibilities. Chapter 1, "What Is So Important About Homework?", serves as an introduction, and Chapter 11, entitled "Still Not Convinced?", concludes the volume.

Part I provides a rationale for meaningful homework, a thumbnail sketch of what some of the leading experts say about homework and authentic learning, and an inside look at why and how the teacher-authors of this text decided to change their homework practices.

Part II focuses on what you—the teacher—can do to make homework more meaningful for your students. It provides preliminary considerations for rethinking homework, offers a meaningful homework-planning guide, illustrates the connection between inquiry skills and meaningful assignments, and presents a rich description of elements that should be thought through at each phase of the homework cycle.

Part III connects you with your students by describing the general nature of the learner at specified grades. Each of the chapters designated by grade levels (early elementary, upper elementary, middle school, and high school) provides homework examples from each of the four core areas (and a smaller selection from the electives). Note that, although these chapters are subdivided by level, we believe that each maintains a degree of universal applicability, so we encourage you to spend some time examining each.

Acknowledgments

We wish to thank the colleagues, students, and teachers who have collaborated with our work and enriched our understanding of classroom teaching and learning. This includes the faculty and staff of the College of Education at Michigan State University, an institution that exemplifies the concept of learning community and nurtures groundbreaking and collaborative work such as ours.

We also wish to express our appreciation to Amy Peebles who provided vital text processing support to the project. She consistently handled manuscript preparation and other normal secretarial tasks with efficiency and good humor.

Although this book is dedicated to Jere Brophy who suddenly passed away shortly after this manuscript was sent to the publisher, we want to acknowledge Jere's spouse, Arlene Pintozzi Brophy, and Janet Alleman's spouse, George Trumbull, for their unwavering patience and support.

Barbara would like to acknowledge the support of her staff and principal at Winans Elementary School. They have provided a wonderful sounding board over the years as she has grown as a teacher. She would particularly like to thank her teaching partners Gini Larson and Nathan Stevenson for picking up the slack when necessary to make sure school runs smoothly. Finally, she must thank her husband, Keith, for all those very late night dinners so she could meet with the rest of the writing team.

Ben would like to acknowledge the unwavering love and support of Kelly, his wife, and two children, William and Izabelle, the three of whom give tirelessly of themselves so that "daddy could chase a dream." Along with his family, Ben would like to acknowledge the support of his colleagues and the principals at Lowell Senior High School. He would particularly like to thank his "west-side" teaching partners—Phil Beachler, Amanda Blyth, Tosha Duczkowski-Oxley, and Amanita Fahrni—whose energy and passion for serving children provided a daily source of inspiration. Thank you!

Rob would like to acknowledge his mom who taught him that being creative comes from a focus on abundance rather than lack. He would like to thank his students, particularly the Flying Squirrels for motivating him to keep it real. He would also like to thank Diane Lindbert, a principal who connects with a teacher's vision and never forgets to put students first. Finally, he would like to thank Dr. Janet Alleman for inspiring him to transform frustrations with education into researchable questions. With Jan, he is always in.

Sarah would like to acknowledge the "basement" crew of TEAM 8B at Owosso Middle School for welcoming her as a first year teacher and for the many ways they mentored and taught her during those early years. She would particularly like to thank Julie Croy and JoDell Heroux for helping her grow as a teacher who advocates for children. Sarah must also thank the two teachers who have made the most distinctive impacts on her teaching, her mom and dad, Rick and Kate Zimbelman, both veteran teachers who are amazing at what they do! Above all, Sarah thanks her husband, Andrew, for his constant support and encouragement over the years, for helping her pursue her passions, and fending for himself for two years of Thursday night dinners. To her children, Elijah and Abigail, may you always find the same joy in learning as you do at ages three and one.

PUBLISHER'S ACKNOWLEDGMENTS

We would like to thank the following reviewers for their contributions:

Regina Brinker, Science teacher
Christensen Middle School,
    Livermore, CA

George Goodfellow, Chemistry Teacher
Scituate High School, North Scituate, RI

Jane Hunn, Science Teacher
Tippecanoe Valley Middle School,
    Akron, IN

Madeleine Janover, Social Studies
    Teacher
Common Ground High School, New
    Haven, CT

Mary Johnstone, Principal
Rabbit Creek School, Anchorage, AK

Jeremy Kennson Dove, Science Teacher
Monticello High School,
    Charlottesville, VA

Eric Kincaid, Biology Teacher
Morgantown High School,
    Morgantown, WV

Sally Koczan, Science Teacher
Wydown Middle School, Clayton, MO

Eric Langhorst, Social Studies Teacher
South Valley Junior High School,
    Liberty, MO

LeAnn Morris, Technology Teacher
Empire Elementary School, Carson
    City, NV

Jessica Purcell, Science Teacher
South Fargo High School, Fargo, ND

Theron J. Schutte, Superintendent
Boone Community School District,
    Boone, IA

Tim Tharrington, English Teacher
Wakefield Middle School, Raleigh, NC

Julie Wakefield, Social Studies Teacher
McQueen High School, Reno, NV

About the Authors

 **Janet Alleman** is a Professor in the Department of Teacher Education at Michigan State University. She is author and coauthor of a range of publications including *Children's Thinking about Cultural Universals* and a three-volume series entitled *Social Studies Excursions, K–3.* In addition to serving on a host of committees at the state and national levels, she has been a classroom and television teacher, actively working in school settings, and has taught at over a dozen international sites.

 **Jere Brophy** was a University Distinguished Professor of Teacher Education and Educational Psychology at Michigan State University. A clinical and developmental psychologist by training, he conducted research on teachers' achievement expectations and related self-fulfilling prophecy effects, teachers' attitudes toward individual students and the dynamics of teacher-student relationships, students' personal characteristics and their effects on teachers, relationships between classroom processes and student achievement, teachers' strategies for managing classrooms and coping with problem students, and teachers' strategies for motivating students to learn. Most recently, he focused on curricular content and instructional method issues involved in teaching social studies for understanding, appreciation, and life application.

 **Ben Botwinski** is currently enrolled as a full-time graduate student at the College of Education, Michigan State University, where he is studying educational policy and administration. Prior to becoming a full-time student, Botwinski served as a high school social studies teacher in west Michigan. He currently lives in East Lansing, Michigan, with his wife and two children.

Barbara Knighton is an elementary school teacher with over 20 years of experience in the classroom, including 16 years concentrating on the early grades. She currently teaches fourth grade in the Waverly Community Schools in Lansing, Michigan. Barbara has coauthored or contributed to several books on education, including two with an in-depth look at teaching in the primary classroom.

Rob Ley has taught third and fourth grade in both urban and suburban districts. He received his BA and MA from Michigan State University and is currently teaching in the Haslett Public Schools in Haslett, Michigan. He has presented research at state and national conferences related to making curriculum more meaningful for students by integrating community resources. He also directs an enrichment cluster learning context that focuses on creating a time and place for real-world, student-driven learning. Outside the classroom, he leads hiking and cycling adventures in various locations throughout the world.

Sarah Middlestead is a middle school teacher with seven years of experience in the mathematics classroom. She obtained both her undergraduate and graduate degrees at Michigan State University and spent the first seven years of her teaching career at a middle school in mid-Michigan. Sarah is passionate about teaching mathematics in an innovative and creative way, guiding students in exploring how mathematics is used in the world in which they live. She is currently enjoying time at home with her two young children while tutoring and writing.

Part I

Realize the Purpose

Part I is intended to provide you with the rationale for meaningful home-work, a thumbnail sketch of what some of the leading experts say about homework, and an inside look at why and how the teacher-authors of this text changed their homework practices.

1

What Is So Important About Homework?

Despite the current craze for standards, testing, and the need to learn more in order to be prepared for life, many students are less than excited about school and are not achieving at higher levels. Even high achievers often appear to be just "doing school"—a term used to describe a school system in which success depends more on going through the correct motions than on learning and engagement (Pope, 2001). Too often, what students are asked to do is neither memorable nor meaningful. One reason is that they find no purpose in what they are being asked to do—they see no relevant connection to their lives. To exacerbate the problem, teachers often abandon exciting and successful units that are not strictly aligned to the standards and assessments.

An important but often overlooked component of the learning cycle is homework. It has been the source of heated debate among educational researchers and practitioners (not to mention parents and students) for decades, but we are convinced that "homework done right" holds enormous promise for helping teachers and students address some of education's most pressing challenges. Our classrooms and students are living proof of what is possible.

Now, we can almost hear you say, "You must be kidding!" We, too, had a litany of frustrations and often felt trapped given the pressures that bubbled up from multiple fronts regarding homework, which in most school systems seems to be viewed as a necessary evil rather than a valuable curriculum component.

Which of our former frustrations are you currently facing?

THAT'S ME!

As a classroom teacher, do any of these scenarios mirror your experiences? If so, we hope this book will motivate you to take steps toward the alleviation of your homework frustrations. Highlight the responses that make you shout, "That's me!"

I seem to get inundated with homework papers to check, so I find myself assigning work that I correct during faculty meetings, or when I'm chilling on the sofa after dinner, or that can be corrected by a volunteer.

With the increased pressure from NCLB, state standards, and the enormous push to cover content, I find myself simply asking students to do at home what we don't complete at school. New content and new skills end up being the norm.

I get so frustrated with the 50 percent who do not bother to turn in their homework—and often fail the course because of it. I feel like a failure.

I'm overwhelmed with keeping up with the district's pacing guide. I have to give homework that will keep us on track with other classes. If I do something different, I'll get behind.

I'm sick of the e-mail questions and complaints from parents about the assignments. You'd think I'd asked them to do the homework.

I forgot it; the dog ate it; my mom forgot to wake me up so I could do it; it's at my Dad's house—the list of excuses goes on and on. Why bother trying to get these kids to live up to my expectations? They simply don't care!

The principal is a stickler about assigning 20 minutes of homework a night for first graders, an hour for sixth graders, etc. It's become a real headache. I admit I do not put a lot of time into figuring out the tasks I assign. I base my assignments on the time I think they will take to complete.

I have to give homework that connects to our district's learning programs or kits. I need to make sure that students are getting practice with the concepts in our math, science, social studies, and literacy programs or else they might not do well on the district and state tests.

I'm pretty sure there are certain cliques that do their homework "cooperatively." With their high-tech savvy, it is so easy.

My students don't know how to do assignments that require learning skills. They don't know how to collect data or ask good interview questions. They and their families need assignments that are very structured or else they won't complete them.

We can have a perfectly engaging class discussion, but the minute I shift to giving the nightly homework assignment, the eyes roll, the nasty whispers begin, and the books slam shut. It's really deflating.

I don't feel confident enough to design assignments that are different from my district's packaged learning curriculum. I need more experience with those units before I can create more meaningful assignments that feel more risky.

Parents complain that they don't see how their kids can ace all the tests, yet get failing grades on their report cards because of the poor showing on homework. They simply don't get it!

I suspect there's a group of parents who do the homework for their kids and simply have the answers recopied.

MEANINGFUL HOMEWORK

We define *meaningful homework* as tasks that enrich the in-school curriculum by challenging students to think deeply about important questions, apply their knowledge and skills toward solving genuine problems, and creating authentic products that will be used in meaningful ways. Furthermore, out-of-school learning opportunities, which we refer to as *homework*, complement what goes on in school by exploiting home and community resources and environments. Many involve activities that are unfeasible or even impossible to do in classrooms or that are not cost-effective given the limited time students spend in the classroom. Yet they are vital components of a well-rounded education because they involve meaningful learning—a key concept related to motivation, which is linked to achievement.

Meaningful homework is oriented toward authentic forms of student achievement as described by Newmann and Wehlage (1993), who use the word *authentic* to distinguish achievement that is significant and meaningful from that which is trivial and useless. They suggest that teachers need to counteract two persistent maladies that make conventional schooling inauthentic: (1) the work students do often does not allow them to use their minds well, and (2) the work has no intrinsic meaning or value to students beyond achieving in school.

To face these challenges head on, Newmann developed seven articulated standards of instruction, which we believe are congruent with our understanding of meaningful homework. We highlight these ideas in Chapter 3 to provide a sense of the broader context within which we have come to understand the importance of meaningful homework. Each standard is a continuous construct that moves from less to more based on quality. By these standards, homework cannot be judged simply with a yes or no.

Additionally, we suggest that meaningful homework should match the goals of the lessons and units and should expand, enrich, or apply what is learned in school. The results should reveal qualitative changes in the ways students view themselves in relationship to the tasks and should motivate students to continue learning.

"We Believe" Statements

To clarify further our definition of *meaningful homework*, we offer the following statements. This list of contentions forms the foundation of our understanding of meaningful homework and has guided the development of this text. We believe that meaningful homework should

- enrich an existing, successful, well-planned curriculum.
- enhance what was learned in school.
- connect to the big ideas from one or more class sessions.
- support, not replace, classroom instruction.
- provide opportunities to apply skills and knowledge learned at school in a real-world setting.
- reinforce connections between learning in class and life at home and in the real world.
- connect to current or future lessons, units, or projects.
- demonstrate authenticity by incorporating one or more of the following: allow students to organize information and consider alternatives, use concepts in a real way and do the work that real people do, address a problem related to the world beyond the classroom, or address an audience beyond the school (Newmann & Wehlage, 1993).
- be collaborative (if appropriate).

- encourage family participation.
- be used in class as a resource.
- facilitate student contributions to the classroom community.
- inform families about their child's learning.
- allow students to exercise choice and have a say in substantive elements of its design.
- generate excitement and genuine interest in learning.
- relate to learning goals and be at an appropriate level of difficulty, be feasible, and be cost-effective (Brophy & Alleman, 1991).

We also believe that teachers who design or assign meaningful homework should

- have a clear and direct influence on every homework assignment.
- model the assignments for students.
- contribute to the classroom learning community by completing the assignment themselves.
- expect diverse responses rather than a single predetermined answer.
- structure and scaffold the assignments for high rates of success.
- share with others and encourage an audience beyond the classroom.
- showcase or celebrate student work in order to increase completion.
- construct assignments for accessibility regardless of socioeconomic status or ability level.
- balance any disadvantages or difficulties students might face.
- include resources (or guidance about where to locate resources) needed for the assignment.
- maintain high homework expectations for *all* students.
- think of homework as an opportunity rather than as a penalty.
- view homework as something successful learners do.

Note: We recognize that there is a need and a place for basic skills practice (rote/reinforcement) at home. This type of homework is different from assignments with real-world connections and applications. In this text, we will refer to the two types of homework as *basic skills practice* and *meaningful homework*.

OUR APPROACH

Currently, homework is on most schools' radar screens due to heightened concerns about accountability. Teachers are increasingly being asked to align curricula to standards, and instuction is in a time crunch due to the number of hours spent on testing. Many feel that the only way they can get through the material is to assign some of it as homework. Also, many claim that homework is necessary for improving student achievement—an assertion that is only partially supported by research. If this description resonates with you, you likely are wondering, "So what am I to do?"

We believe that homework is—and will continue to be—an integral part of the schooling process. Our approach calls for opening the realm of possibilities for homework with an emphasis on qualitative changes in the way students view themselves in relation to the task (Kohn, 2007). It focuses students on what they are doing, what they are learning in school, and how they can create meaning and apply or extend it in their lives outside of school. In our opinion, homework should be geared toward high-quality learning that engenders in students a continuing desire to gain knowledge.

We suggest that homework practices be viewed as a continuum; thus, even incremental changes toward meaningfulness and authenticity have merit and therefore should be encouraged and supported.

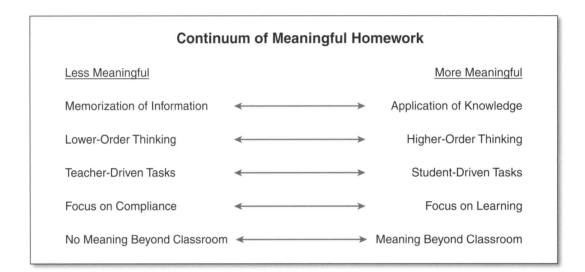

OVERVIEW OF THE TEXT

Your views about homework have been shaped by your personal experiences. So while you might feel forced to buy into your local school policies, in reality your behavior might be (unintentionally) a form of "doing school." The intent of this book is to help you reconcile the issues surrounding homework, sharpen your beliefs about it, negotiate potential roadblocks, better understand the "whys," and entertain the possibility of supplementing or replacing what you do currently with something else you would be willing to try. Think of this initiative as an *experiment.* Be patient! Change doesn't occur quickly. Shifting the homework paradigm begins with you rethinking its purposes, functions, and possibilities. Then you can start educating students, the principal, and families about the "new blend" that takes advantage of the time students spend outside the classroom and strategically engages them in opportunities that validate the in-school content, enhance and expand it, and use the homework results to enliven subsequent in-class activities.

Start small! For example, suppose the goal is for students to learn the states and their capitals. Turn the "ugh" into a scavenger hunt. Provide students with a simple outline map of the United States and ask them to watch the national news for a week, skim newspapers and magazines, listen to the radio while riding in a vehicle, etc., plotting the states and capitals that are mentioned. Then up the ante by asking them to categorize the stories by type: health, disaster, political, economic, human interest, etc. After a week, have students bring their data to school for class conversation, encouraging individualization in its representation. What patterns emerge? What states and capitals were most represented? Least represented? Within what contexts were they mentioned? Encourage students to find additional media sources where states and capitals may be represented. Encourage family involvement.

At some point, you may still feel compelled to quiz students on states and capitals. However, students will have begun to use the information, and they will gradually realize its value in becoming an educated person. A class conversation about the application of geographic facts in one's personal and professional life could spur this process.

REFERENCES

Brophy, J., & Alleman, J. (1991). Activities as instructional tools: A framework for analysis and evaluation. *Educational Researcher, 20,* 9–23.

Kohn, A. (2007). *The homework myth.* Cambridge, MA: DaCapo Press.

Newmann, F., & Wehlage, G. (1993). Five standards of authentic instruction. *Educational Leadership, 50,* 8–12.

Pope, D. C. (2001). *"Doing school": How we are creating a generation of stressed out, materialistic, and mis-educated students.* New Haven, CT: Yale University Press.

2

What Is the Rationale for Homework?

INTRODUCTION

Given the age-grading system, the pressures associated with high-stakes testing, the high student-to-teacher ratio, the ambiguity and risk involved in academic work (Doyle, 1983), and the other features built into mass education systems, students' learning opportunities in classrooms are necessarily limited and somewhat artificial compared to what is possible under more natural and unconstrained conditions. One way for teachers to compensate for this is to use the community as a living laboratory for learning and, in the process, use the diversity of student backgrounds represented in the class for promoting understandings in social studies, science, mathematics, literacy, or other subjects.

PRINCIPLES OF MEANINGFUL HOMEWORK

We have identified several principles of meaningful homework. These principles (sometimes known as purposes or functions) are not presented in any particular order because their relative value depends on the teacher's hierarchy of subject matter goals.

Providing for Expanded Meaningfulness and Life Application of School Learning

Home assignments offer daily opportunities to use what is learned in school in out-of-school settings. For example, goals for a government unit might include helping students to understand and appreciate the value and importance of government regulations in their lives and become more aware of the written and unwritten rules and laws that are a part of their environment. Students could be encouraged to write a journal entry or compose an essay about government regulations for family members and then discuss and look for examples of rules and laws that are part of the household. For elementary students, a "means and functions chart" with examples could be sent home as a resource for use in completing the assignment. Examples of means of governing might include traffic lights, clothing labels, money (since government manufactures the coins and bills we use), drivers' licenses, seat belts, restaurant or meat inspection labels, etc.

Another example for expanding meaningfulness comes from a science unit on conservation. Typical goals might include understanding and appreciating the types of conservation that families, businesses, and communities might consider in order to preserve nonrenewable resources. As a follow-up to lessons focusing on renewable and nonrenewable resources, students could be asked to talk with family members, business owners, or community service personnel about what they might do to conserve nonrenewable resources. Students would be encouraged to bring their lists to school, accompanied by paragraphs explaining what would need to be done to conserve the nonrenewable resources and what changes would be needed to help people agree to do so. Subsequently, a debate might be held as a means of thinking more deeply about related issues, such as offshore drilling.

Constructing Meaning in Natural Ways and Expanding a Sense of Self-Efficacy

Homework opportunities that focus on unit goals provide a natural mechanism for situated learning and for social construction of what students are learning in school. This challenges them to use higher-order thinking as they apply learning to real-world settings. Home assignments can provide natural opportunities for students to contribute ideas and sometimes even educate their families as they examine choices and trade-offs that influence their social experiences and decisions. For example, in a math unit on budgeting, one of the goals might focus on economic decision making (e.g., what constitutes a "good buy"). A homework assignment might address issues such as how families decide whether a grocery store sale on meat is really a good deal as well as the implications of the decision. In a science unit on water conservation, one of the goals might be heightening awareness of the importance of water, the amount used by individuals in their daily lives, and the associated costs and considering what we might do to conserve water. Students and their families could monitor their water usage for a specified time and determine the costs associated with it. After gathering and analyzing their data, families could develop plans for modifying their practices. The plans could then be shared with the class. Once the plans are enacted and new data are gathered and analyzed, the results could be revisited and changes could be discussed.

Students will begin to feel empowered, seeing that they can make a difference using what they have learned. They will begin to realize they can do it—they can contribute, they can decide, they can figure it out. Teachers and families can provide information and opportunities to help students make intelligent decisions in the real world and begin to understand and explain why things are as they are and how they came to be. These experiences develop students' self-efficacy perceptions concerning their knowledge and self-regulation potential in the social domain (Alleman & Brophy, 2000).

Extending Education to the Home and Community by Engaging Adults in Interesting and Responsible Ways

Parents usually value becoming involved with their child's learning in meaningful ways. We typically associate meaningful parental involvement with elementary students and with families that have adequate resources or that at least place a priority on education. However, this same attitude and level of parental engagement can continue through high school if teachers guide adults through the process early on (if necessary) and provide inexpensive resources to make activities easy. For example, providing families with simple maps, timelines, recycled magazines, case studies, simulations/games, disposable cameras, etc. can facilitate gathering information about such things as family histories, current events, proposed family vacations, patterns of human behavior, inventions, signage, or patterns of changes in how specific things are done.

Science, social studies, math, and literacy are all rich with opportunities for involving students in collaborations with family members and the community that can be mutually satisfying and stimulating. Parents, older siblings, babysitters, family friends, neighbors, business owners, factory workers, scientists, city planners, politicians, etc. can be great collaborators for learning without special preparation. The key to success is careful selection of home assignments that reflect the goals of the unit or lesson.

For example, in a class studying safety, one of the goals might be to develop an appreciation of the importance of home safety in an age when many children spend considerable time alone. A powerful out-of-school activity could call for students to conduct home safety surveys with assistance from people available in the household. Using the data, follow-up with in-class structured discourse (a powerful and authentic literacy connection) could provide guidance for how students themselves might respond to their home safety needs and alert family members about other areas needing attention. Students could be encouraged to collect literature in guiding the proposed changes.

In a science unit on the environment, the goals might include understanding relationships of natural phenomena to industries and appreciating the pros and cons of human manipulation of the environment. Here, the teacher could encourage students to ask and discuss with family members or business acquaintances how they have experienced manipulation of the environment in their daily lives, such as during a vacation at a mountain resort or on the job (e.g., construction workers involved in building a new subdivision). In addition to involving adults in meaningful ways, this activity provides opportunities for students to engage in literacy in authentic contexts. Students could be encouraged to bring taped interviews, photographs, postcards, digital photos and stories, or newspaper articles as documentation of their experiences.

Collaborative learning with adults that occurs outside the classroom has the potential for improving in-class participation. Students typically are excited to report the ideas shared by adults, and they begin to see real-world applications. They become involved with their parents and other adults in positive and productive relationships, and as a bonus, these adults will have opportunities to enjoy nonthreatening, rewarding involvement with their child's education.

Taking Advantage of the Students' Diversity by Using It as a Learning Resource

Too often, differences among students are viewed as problems or potential barriers to success. However, these differences can be viewed as opportunities for students to begin with what they know best and link their knowledge to the experiences of others. Having students gather data about their own families to share with peers can create immediate interest in an otherwise too familiar topic. For example, students who live within extended family arrangements could develop responses to a list of questions such as these:

- What role does Grandmother play when Mother works nights?
- How is her role different from what it would be if she lived out of state?
- How do economic conditions affect living conditions (e.g., Are any young adults returning to live with the family due to job losses)?
- What are the domestic benefits of the extended family arrangement?
- What potential challenges need to be worked out?
- How is your living arrangement similar or dissimilar to the one of the family in Japan you read about?

These attributes of one child's extended family can be compared to those of nuclear families and to those of extended families of children from other cultures, noting similarities as well as differences.

Data gathered from family members can also enhance students' appreciation of diverse perspectives and engender the realization that social issues are frequently open to debate. For example, suppose one of the goals of a social studies unit is for the students to understand and appreciate the global connections between their community and East Asia. Typically, students would be asked to read textbook material, discuss it in class, and list connections on the overhead. However, this lesson would have more impact if students were asked first to interview the adults in their households or neighborhoods about their views of global connections with East Asia. For example, a parent or neighbor who is presently laid off from an automobile plant might feel quite differently than a parent or neighbor who sells Japanese-made audio/video equipment at an appliance store. Interviewing could be coupled with an investigation of the home to determine the number and nature of goods from East Asia that are found there. Homes with access to the Internet could provide still another rich resource and serve to illustrate the nearness of places formerly considered remote. The data then could be funneled back into the classroom to aid students in achieving the "documented" realization that local beliefs and values about globalization are tied to people's life experiences. The net result could be a memorable unit that incorporates a host of literacy opportunities and expands students' knowledge and appreciation of multiple views.

Diverse perspectives in science can be equally compelling. For example, in a unit focusing on cells, students could be asked to elicit opinions from family members and other adults on the topic of stem cell research. What are people's views within our community, and why do they have them? Class discussion would provide a safe venue for exploring multiple perspectives. The teacher could expose students to ideas that might be challenged by family members if assigned as content to be read at home. Note that in such a teaching situation, finding a balanced set of articles from a range of legitimate sources and at the appropriate reading level can be challenging but is nonetheless essential.

These out-of-school learning experiences can be rewarding for all the individuals involved, and the data that are "harvested" during follow-up discussions can be provocative, insightful, and rich in diverse perspectives and examples.

Personalizing the Curriculum and Reflecting on the Here and Now

Home assignments can enhance students' awareness and understanding of the contexts of their daily lives and the lives of their families. They begin to realize that the curriculum can be dynamic. It is not simply material from a book that needs to be read, discussed, and tested. It can be personal and contemporary.

In a literacy unit on communication or journalism, a goal might be to develop students' awareness of how they spend their out-of-school time and, in particular, how much of each week is spent with mass communication. Class members, with the assistance of family members, could be asked to monitor their television viewing using a form provided for easy recording. The data could be used to construct a graph of students' television viewing and inform a subsequent discussion of the results (Alleman & Brophy, 2003).

Another goal of the same unit might be to develop an understanding and appreciation of the variety of ways in which television influences its viewers. After learning about commercials and advertising techniques, students could write letters to their families (or if they are older, conduct a workshop for parents), informing them about the important things they learned and making at least one recommendation to consider during future viewing. Appropriate recommendations might include (a) "Don't believe everything the commercials tell you," or (b) "Some sports shoes cost a lot more than other brands because the companies pay popular sports figures to advertise their product, so make sure those shoes are really worth the extra dollars." Students could also ask their families to discuss how commercials had influenced them and what new questions they might want to ask before they purchase advertised products. Families could be encouraged to "test" the accuracy of the commercials. The results, when shared in the classroom, could stimulate spirited discussion.

Exploiting Learning Opportunities That Are Not Cost-Effective on School Time

Students' homes and the surrounding community are filled with learning resources that might not be cost-effective for exploitation during an organized field trip. However, such resources could be explored by one or more individuals who might be asked to visit a particular site and report back to class. For example, suppose that an intermediate-grade or high school class were going to study local government. It might not be feasible for the whole class to attend a city council meeting, but a few students and their families could volunteer to do so. They could serve as observers, data gatherers, and primary sources for a follow-up in-class discussion. The entire class would be involved in the initial reading and planning, and then the active student participants would go to the session armed with questions from their peers and return having fulfilled a class mission. The follow-up discussion could address the preliminary peer questions and the participants' observations. Students would be expected to take turns going on special assignments with their parents so that their classmates could benefit from a range of field trips that would not be feasible within the parameters of most school budgets.

As a second example, suppose a class was studying government with special attention to rules and laws. Taking the whole class on a walking tour of the community looking for signs of unwritten and written rules and laws might be too time-consuming, but this task could be a very productive and challenging use of afterschool time. Students could easily combine this assignment with the regular school bus ride or walk home. For best results, the teacher should provide a data-retrieval form so that the next day's discussion is not based simply on memory.

Another example of a homework opportunity that would not be cost-effective if done during school time, yet could be useful when structured appropriately and tied to in-school goals, is watching a specific television show. The teacher could instruct students to watch a show with an eye toward understanding gender roles or acquiring knowledge and appreciation of a particular place, issue, or group of people (e.g., gun control or women in Islamic countries). Additional examples might include attending a community meeting focused on a heated topic such as zoning, environmentally sensitive issues, or building a water treatment plant and interviewing meeting participants to document their opinions on the issue. These out-of-school learning opportunities expand students' learning horizons, serve as validity checks for book learning, and provide authentic connections that extend beyond the school day.

Keeping the Curriculum Up-to-Date

K–12 social studies textbooks are often years out-of-date on world events. In such cases, it is important to supplement the text with home assignments involving newspapers, magazines, television broadcasts, and Internet linkages. The additional information can be used to inform discussions of the changes occurring and the challenges created by new conditions. Instead of only reading outdated material regarding U.S. leadership and our country's affairs, students can learn at the cutting edge of national and world developments. For example, discussion could focus on the effects of the events of 9/11. How has our country changed since that historical event? If students engage adults in their households or neighborhoods in discussion of such questions, those adults may come to view their children in a new light, and children and adults may engage in a cross-generational dialogue about a topic of real interest.

Math, science, and literacy are less time-sensitive than social studies; nonetheless, the examples used to illustrate the skills, central questions, big ideas, etc. quickly become outdated. Also, the use of newspapers, television, magazines, and Internet linkages (including podcasts, etc.) to address the here and now speaks to the "need to know" issue that teachers are often challenged to answer as justification for assignments.

TEACHER AND FAMILY INVOLVEMENT

Home assignments are one way for teachers to model and establish the norm that everybody has the opportunity to learn outside of school. We observed one student exclaim to the teacher, "You're doing the homework too!" The teacher explained that she also was learning new things about her community. On another occasion, a student with a rather puzzled look said, "I thought you just cooked up things to keep us busy. Look, you're doing them too!" Soon students come to realize that if the teacher participates in home assignments and actually brings data back to the class to share, the assignments must be important.

Having the teacher model returning home assignments is a good way to overcome one of the teacher's motivational concerns. Another concern relates to family willingness to participate in home learning opportunities. Many think that helping their child is cheating, or that they may not know the right answer, or that they simply don't have the time to help, or that it's the teacher's job to educate their child. Overcoming these obstacles requires ongoing education about the power of meaningful learning outside of school and the role families can play in enhancing student interest in curriculum content and influencing student achievement. It requires explaining to families through letters, conferences, e-mails, telephone conversations, and public presentations how they can help their children, why they should help their children, and the rationale for meaningful home assignments.

REFERENCES

Alleman, J., & Brophy, J. (2000). On the menu: The growth of self-efficacy. *Social Studies and the Young Learner, 12*(3), 15–19.

Alleman, J., & Brophy, J. (2003). History is alive: Teaching your children about changes over time. *The Social Studies, 94*, 107–110.

Doyle, W. (1983). Academic work. *Review of Educational Research, 53*, 159–199.

3

What Do the Experts Say About Homework?

INTRODUCTION

The purpose of this chapter is to link two topics that traditionally have been separate entities: homework and opportunities for authentic learning. How can we as educators make our homework assignments authentic learning? Current professional literature does not discuss meaningful homework as an authentic learning experience. We will look at these two topics separately in this chapter and then make explicit connections in the remainder of the text.

The homework section begins with a general overview followed by a brief history of homework. It considers both the positive and the negative aspects of homework. Note, however, that within the studies cited, no distinction was made between well-designed and poorly designed homework. We contend that there are differences in the effectiveness of homework based on two factors: its nature and its design.

The authentic learning section includes definitions of authenticity, the nature of authentic tasks, and arguments for and against authentic learning. While the authentic learning literature is not specific to homework, these principles apply to the design of meaningful homework.

HOMEWORK

General Overview

Homework has been evaluated from as early as the 1930s, and opinions about its value have been in constant flux. Early in the 20th century, the common belief among educators was that homework helped to create disciplined minds. However, by 1940, the idea of homework began to have negative connotations, as it was believed to interfere with the home and family life of students. Then with the launch of the

Soviet *Sputnik* in the 1950s, the rigor of American schools was brought into question. In an effort to enhance the mathematics and science achievement of American students, more rigorous homework was again introduced as a partial solution to beating the Soviets in the space race. But by the 1980s, the homework trend had reversed again, with some learning theorists claiming that homework could be detrimental to students' mental health (Marzano & Pickering, 2007b). The debate continues today, as impassioned arguments for and against homework are returning to the forefront of the educational community.

Homework traditionally is defined as "tasks assigned to students by school teachers that are intended to be carried out during nonschool hours" (Cooper, 1994, p. 2). Cooper has classified homework according to its amount, purpose, skill area, degree of individualization, degree of choice for the student, completion deadline, and social context.

Positive Aspects of Homework

Homework is a potentially powerful instructional tool. Harris Cooper (1989) cites the positive effects of homework as "(a) immediate academic effects, (b) long-term academic effects, (c) nonacademic effects, and (d) parental involvement effects" (p. 10). Among these claimed effects, Cooper says that "the immediate effects of homework on learning are the most frequent rationales for assigning it" (p. 6). To proponents, it makes logical sense that assigning homework increases the amount of time that a student spends on academic tasks because it extends learning beyond the school day. Typically, students in countries such as Japan, Germany, and France academically outperform American students (Marzano & Pickering, 2007b). This could be attributed to the fact that students overseas spend twice as much time on demanding content as their American counterparts (Marzano & Pickering).

Numerous studies report that homework has a positive effect on student achievement. Seventeen research reports dating back to 1962 compared classrooms that assigned homework to those that did not. The reports encompassed over 3,300 students in 11 states from 30 schools and 85 classrooms. In the studies, 48 comparisons were found, of which 18 involved class tests or grades and 30 involved standardized achievement tests (Cooper, 1994). The following conclusions can be drawn (Cooper, 1994):

- Of the comparisons, 70 percent indicated that homework had a positive effect on student achievement.
- Of students completing homework, 55 percent had higher achievement scores than students not doing homework.
- The positive effect of homework varies across grade levels. In Grades 4 to 6, students who did homework outscored 52 percent of students not doing homework. Middle school students doing homework outscored 60 percent of students not doing homework. High school students doing homework outscored 69 percent of students not doing homework.
- No consistent patterns have been found in comparisons between males and females.
- Subject matter influenced the comparisons slightly. Mathematics showed the smallest effect from homework, with reading and English in the middle, and science and social studies showing the largest effect.

- Specifically in mathematics, problem solving revealed less of a homework effect than other mathematical skills.
- Homework had larger effects when achievement was measured using grades or class tests as opposed to standardized tests.
- Shorter but more frequent homework assignments (i.e., more assignments per week) showed the greatest effect.
- The effect of homework was larger in studies where the researcher also was the teacher.

Marzano and Pickering (2007b) summarized Cooper, Robinson, and Patall's 2006 comparison of homework versus no homework by saying that

> the average student in a class in which appropriate homework was assigned would score 23 percentile points higher on tests of the knowledge addressed in that class than the average student in a class in which homework was not assigned. (p. 75)

Even among researchers who support the use of homework, the literature does suggest discrepancies. One topic under debate is the impact that time spent on homework has on student achievement. Some researchers claim that as time spent on homework increases, student achievement will also increase. For example, in a very general sense, Marzano and Pickering (2007b) said that for middle school students, the benefits of homework "increased as time increased, up to one to two hours of homework a night, and then decreased" (p. 75). More specifically, Cooper (1989) said that the relationship between time on homework and achievement is curvilinear:

> For high school students the positive relation between the variables does not appear until at least one hour of homework per week is reported. Then it continues to climb unabated to the highest interval. On the other hand, for junior high students the positive relation appears for even the most minimal level of time spent on homework, but it disappears entirely at the highest interval. (p. 108)

On the other hand, substantial literature suggests that time spent on homework is not an accurate indicator of achievement. According to Trautwein, Ludtke, Kastens, and Koller (2006),

> several recent studies that have separated the effects of homework assignment and homework completion indicate that students who spend more time on homework do not necessarily outperform their peers (De Jong, Westerhof, & Creemers, 2000; Muhlenbruck et al., 2000; Trautwein, in press). . . . In fact, *effort* invested in homework has proved to have a more consistently positive impact on achievement gains than has time on homework. (p. 1094)

Trautwein et al. (2006) go on to conclude that "homework effort and homework time were almost completely unrelated. This result corroborates the view that homework time should not be used as a measure of students' investment in school" (p. 1100).

Marzano and Pickering (2007b) agree:

Focusing on the amount of time students spend on homework may miss the point. A significant proportion of the research on homework indicates that the positive effects of homework relate to the amount of homework that the student *completes* rather than the amount of time spent on homework or the amount of homework actually assigned. (p. 77)

They summarize the case for homework as follows:

Appropriate homework must be structured in a way that students can accomplish it with relatively high success rates, so that they will complete all or large portions of the homework. This is not a simple or straightforward task. We can hope that, in the near future, research will bring into sharper focus exactly what the characteristics of effective homework are. In the meantime, educators can and should continue to assign homework, but they should do so in a manner that is well thought out and produces discernible results in student achievement. In the absence of these characteristics, homework should not be assigned simply as a matter of routine. (Marzano & Pickering, 2007a, p. 513)

Negative Aspects of Homework

Arguments against homework are becoming increasingly prevalent in today's society. Anti-homework authors claim that the research supporting homework has been poorly conducted, riddled with bias, or simply not convincing. Kralovec and Buell (2000) said that "we have been led to believe that homework helps boost academic achievement. In fact, findings on the relationship between homework time and academic achievement are conflicting and misleading" (p. 11). Similarly, Kohn (2006) stated that Cooper's studies reveal "further examples of his determination to massage the numbers until they yield something—anything—on which to construct a defense of homework for younger children" (p. 84). Kohn said that the research misrepresents the actual impact of homework:

In studies that involve in-class tests, some students are given homework—which usually consists of reviewing a batch of facts about some topic—and then they, along with their peers who didn't get the homework, take a quiz on that very material. The outcome measure, in other words, is precisely aligned to the homework that some students did and other didn't do—or that they did in varying amounts. It's as if you were told to spend time in the evening learning the names of all the vice presidents of the United States and were then tested only on those names. If you remembered more of them after cramming, the researcher would then conclude that "learning in the evening" is effective. (pp. 31–32)

Kohn (2006) also argued that the research advocating the use of homework is inaccurate because course grades are used to determine whether homework made a difference in achievement. The literature suggests that it would be natural for achievement to increase if the same teacher writes the homework and the tests. If the homework is directly related to the test, and more homework is done, grades will also increase. Kohn wrote, "The studies that use grades as the outcome measure, not surprisingly, tend to show a much stronger effect for homework than studies that use standardized test scores" (p. 32).

Harris Cooper (1989) cites the following as being negative aspects of homework: (a) satiation, (b) denial of access to leisure time and community activities, (c) parental interference, (d) cheating, and (e) increased difference between high and low achievers. A common thread in the literature opposing homework is that homework practices widen the gap between privileged and disadvantaged students. According to Kralovec and Buell (2000), "Homework is a practice that perpetuates the social-class inequity that seems to be built into schooling. When we look at homework in the context of a poor student's life, the practice seems almost abusive" (p. 80). These authors went on to say that "we must acknowledge that students return home to very different environments with vastly different resources. Homework takes time, space, study aids, and very particular academic skills, resources that are by no means equally distributed across American communities" (p. 80). They asserted that homework unintentionally penalizes economically disadvantaged students because their lives at home make it virtually impossible to complete homework, stating, "If we all need a quiet well-lit place to study, far away from the TV, we would like to suggest that we know a perfect spot that precisely meets those requirements: the schoolhouse" (p. 80).

To level the playing field between advantaged and disadvantaged students, the anti-homework literature suggests lengthening the school day so that all students may have a chance to complete homework before they return to their varying home lives (Kohn, 2006; Wallis, 2006). Kohn said that

> if higher test scores were associated with a heavier homework load, it would probably be due to the fact that both are correlated with higher socioeconomic status, not because assigning more homework *caused* the test scores to rise. In fact, when wealth is held constant, the two may not even be related. (p. 130)

The literature very strongly suggests that homework (as typically conceived) is not equitable and accessible to all students.

The literature also suggests that homework has the potential to create tension between students and their parents. Kohn (2006) cited one study in which more than a third of fifth graders said they "get tense working with their parents on homework" (p. 13). A survey of over 1,200 parents of kindergartners through 12th graders showed that half of the parents reported "they had had a serious argument with their child about homework in the past year that involved yelling or crying" (Kohn, p. 13). In a *Time* article, journalist Claudia Wallis (2006) recalled the following scene from her home:

> My 12-year-old daughter and I had been drilling social-studies key words for more than an hour. It was 11 P.M. Our entire evening had, as usual, consisted of homework and conversations (a.k.a. nagging) about homework. She was tired and fed up. I was tired and fed up. The words wouldn't stick. They meant nothing to her. They didn't mean much to me either. (¶ 1)

This is a familiar scene in many American homes. Homework opponents argue that the parent-child relationship is difficult enough without adding tension over homework. In addition, homework forces parents to be teachers when that is not their job. According to Kralovec and Buell (2000),

> As parents we are led to ask, whose job is it to teach our children? Some of us see such homework assignments not as a sign that the school is doing a good job, but rather as an indication that it has ceded it responsibility for teaching to the parents. (p. 15)

The anti-homework literature also suggests that the amount of homework assigned is so great that it is robbing our students of their childhood. Kohn (2006) said that

> the most striking trend regarding homework in the past two decades is the tendency to pile more and more of it on younger and younger children. . . . Today it is the rare educator who is brave enough to question whether first graders really need to fill out worksheets at home. (p. 6)

The literature suggests that one reason for this increase in the amount of homework is that schools are becoming increasingly departmentalized in earlier grades. In these cases, teachers assign homework without knowing how much has already been given in the other subjects.

As the amount of homework increases, opponents are becoming more vocal. According to the director of the Golden Independent School in Colorado,

> six and a half hours a day in school is enough. . . . Kids and families need the rest of the days/evenings/weekends/holidays for living—playing, having friends and pets, shopping, solving problems, cooking, eating, chores, traveling, playing on sports teams, communicating, finding out about world news, playing musical instruments, reading for pleasure, watching movies, collecting things, etc., etc., etc. (Erika Sueker, as quoted by Kohn, 2006, p. 16)

Children are losing opportunities to do things that they ought to be able to do. They are losing time with their families and opportunities to pursue hobbies of their own interest. There is less time to just be a child given the increasing amount of homework and the burden that it places on families. Kralovec and Buell (2000) claimed that homework "interferes with important family and community participation" (p. 22). The literature resounds with the idea that any time spent doing homework is time that is *not* spent doing other, more valuable things.

> To what extent do we believe children (and families) should be able to decide how to spend their time together? For that matter, what do we think childhood ought to be about? To require students to do homework on a regular basis is to give one kind of answer to these questions. (Kohn, 2006, p. 17)

Another claim is that homework is a sure-fire way to squelch a love of learning among students. Kohn (2006) said, "Most kids hate homework. They dread it, groan about it, put off doing it as long as possible. It may be the single most reliable extinguisher of the flame of curiosity" (p. 17).

While the literature is inconclusive regarding the costs/benefits of homework, the reality is that many teachers assign it and school districts require it. Therefore, informed teachers need to make thoughtful decisions about how to design meaningful homework that will benefit both students and their families.

Homework Guidelines

"Research provides some evidence that, when used appropriately, homework benefits student achievement" (Marzano & Pickering, 2007b, p. 76). In fact, homework assignments can be viewed as "opportunities to expand and enrich the curriculum" (Brophy & Alleman, 2007, p. 265). Though the literature suggests that homework can be beneficial, researchers caution that it must be appropriate. "Homework must be realistic in length and difficulty given the students' abilities to work independently" (Good & Brophy, 2008, p. 394). Brophy and Alleman (2007) also offered four primary criteria that must be met by all meaningful homework activities: (a) goal relevance, (b) appropriate level of difficulty, (c) feasibility, and (d) cost.

Educators are also cautioned that "even for these oldest students, too much homework may diminish its effectiveness or even become counterproductive" (Cooper, Robinson, & Patall, 2006, p. 53). Based on research findings, Cooper (cited in Marzano & Pickering, 2007b) suggested using the "10-minute rule," which states that the combined amount of homework should take about as long to complete as 10 minutes multiplied by the student's grade level. For example, an eighth-grade student should not be expected to complete more than 80 minutes (8th grade times 10 minutes) per night. Even some homework critics believe that a sensible homework policy could be based on this 10-minute rule (Wallis, 2006). Marzano and Pickering (2007b) suggested the following research-based homework guidelines (p. 79):

- Assign purposeful homework.
- Design homework to maximize the chances that students will complete it.
- Involve parents in appropriate ways.
- Carefully monitor the amount of homework assigned.

AUTHENTIC LEARNING

Authentic learning is a broad and diverse topic that cannot be addressed in just a few paragraphs. However, having some foundational knowledge of authentic education will assist you in your exploration of meaningful homework.

Definitions

Authentic learning has been defined in multiple ways:

- "Student engagement in ideas, concepts, skills, and activities that mean something to them and that lead both to a deeper understanding and to the ability to put ideas to work" (Fried, 2005, p. x).
- "The idea of learning in contexts that promote real-life applications of knowledge . . . help learners integrate needed knowledge, skills and attitudes, coordinate individual skills that comprise a complex task, and transfer their school learning to life or work settings" (Rule, 2006, p. 1).

- "Refers to something being genuine rather than artificial or misleading" (Newmann, 1996, p. 282).
- "The vehicle through which everything from basic skills to advanced content and processes come together in the form of student-developed products and services" (Renzulli, Gentry, & Reis, 2004, p. 74).

Five commonalities emerge from the varying definitions:

1. Authentic learning means something to the student.

2. Authentic learning engages students.

3. Authentic learning leads to deep, as opposed to superficial, knowledge.

4. Authentic learning offers opportunities to solve problems in a real-world context.

5. Authentic learning provides choice for students.

Pedagogical practices that are grounded in the concept of authentic learning offer alternatives to the ways in which teaching and learning processes are traditionally conceived. Fried (2005) said that in a traditional school setting, "the dominant instructional strategy is one of teachers telling students what they think students need to know" (p. 129). In contrast, in an authentic learning setting, "the dominant instructional strategy involves teachers asking students to explore with them what they believe is important for students to learn" (p. 129). The difference between these two statements holds important implications for the classroom and suggests that there is a wide gap between classrooms that foster authentic learning and those that do not.

The Nature of Authentic Tasks

According to Newmann (1996), if a task is to be authentic and foster authentic learning, three criteria must be achieved: (a) construction of knowledge, (b) disciplined inquiry, and (c) value beyond school (p. 22). Newmann further developed these three components of authenticity by breaking them down into seven standards by which authentic tasks can be measured. These standards may be applied to measure the authenticity of any tasks used either inside or outside of the classroom. (Newmann, p. 29):

- Construction of knowledge
  Standard 1: Organization of information. The task asks students to organize, synthesize, interpret, explain, or evaluate complex information in addressing a concept, problem, or issue.
  Standard 2: Consideration of alternatives. The task asks students to consider alternative solutions, strategies, perspectives, or points of view in addressing a concept, problem, or issue.

- Disciplined inquiry
  Standard 3: Disciplinary content. The task asks students to show understanding and/or to use ideas, theories, or perspectives considered central to an academic or professional discipline.

Standard 4: Disciplinary process. The task asks students to use methods of inquiry, research, or communication characteristic of an academic or professional discipline.

Standard 5: Elaborated written communication. The task asks students to elaborate on their understanding, explanations, or conclusions through extended writing.

- Value beyond school

Standard 6: Problem connected to the world beyond the classroom. The task asks students to address a concept, problem, or issue that is similar to one that they have encountered or are likely to encounter in life beyond the classroom.

Standard 7: Audience beyond the school. The task asks students to communicate their knowledge, present a product or performance, or take some action for an audience beyond the teacher, classroom, and school building.

Newmann (1996) noted that it is ideal to strive for each of the three components of authenticity but that instruction and assessment may not meet all three at the same time. "The point is not to abandon all traditional forms of schoolwork, but to keep authentic achievement clearly in view as the valued end" (p. 288).

In addition to Newmann's standards, the Center for Authentic Task Design (2005) lists the following criteria for authentic tasks:

- Have real-world relevance.
- Are ill defined, requiring students to define the tasks and subtasks needed to complete the activity.
- Comprise complex tasks to be investigated by students over a sustained period of time.
- Provide the opportunity for students to examine the task from different perspectives, using a variety of resources.
- Provide the opportunity to collaborate.
- Provide the opportunity to reflect.
- Can be integrated and applied across different subject areas and lead beyond domain-specific outcomes.
- Are seamlessly integrated with assessment.
- Create polished products valuable in their own right rather than as preparation for something else.
- Allow competing solutions and diversity of outcomes.

Some authorities suggest that a critical component of authentic learning should include the solving of real-life problems. Real-life problems possess the following four features:

1. The problems must have personal meaning for the student. "The problem must involve an emotional or internal commitment on the part of those involved in addition to a cognitive interest."

2. "No agreed-on solutions or prescribed strategies for solving the problem exist."

3. The problems "motivate people to find solutions that change actions, attitudes, or beliefs."

4. The problems must "target a real audience" (Renzulli et al., 2004, p. 74).

Arguments Against Authentic Learning

Authentic learning has been claimed to "neglect the teaching of basic skills or important content that will handicap students when taking tests required for college admission" (Newmann, 1996, p. 43). In response to the claim, Newmann cited the following studies that show the results of teaching for understanding and authentic learning instead of memorization of facts and algorithms:

- Michael S. Knapp, in 140 classrooms in 15 elementary schools that served disadvantaged students, found that these students "consistently outperformed students in more conventional classrooms on advanced skills and did as well as or better on traditional tests (Knapp, as cited in Newmann, 1996, p. 43).
- "Studies of mathematics in grades 1, 2, and 8 offer further evidence that instruction consistent with some of these authentic standards benefits students on conventional measures of achievement" (Newmann, 1996, p. 43).
- In Newmann's own study of restructured schools, it was found that student in schools "demonstrating the highest levels of authentic pedagogy performed as well as or better than other comparable students in terms of standardized tests scores" (Newmann, 1996, p. 43).
- In another study, Newmann, Marks, and Gamoran (1996) found that "regardless of race or gender, an average student would increase from about the thirtieth percentile to about the sixtieth percentile [on NEAP achievements tests] as a result of exposure to high rather than low levels of authentic pedagogy" (p. 302).

Another criticism of authenticity is a belief that if authentic student performance is the focus, some important content will be eliminated from the curriculum. While content continues to be in flux, these curricular decisions remain in the hands of educators, policymakers, and the public to decide.

CONCLUSION

We believe that homework can be an essential part of the curriculum, enhancing students' understanding of course content if it is made to be meaningful. As evidenced by the literature, there are both positives and negatives associated with homework. We believe that when homework is appropriately designed and meaningful to the student, the good will outweigh the bad. Principles of authentic learning can be used to help design meaningful homework. In essence, if we are to make our homework meaningful to students, it must be rooted in the ideas of authenticity. Join us in the rest of this book as we discuss what meaningful homework looks like, how it impacts students, and how it supports your instruction.

REFERENCES

Brophy, J., & Alleman, J. (2007). *Powerful social studies for elementary students* (2nd ed.). Belmont, CA: Thomson-Wadsworth.

Center for Authentic Task Design. (2005). *Authentic task design.* Retrieved December 30, 2009, from the University of Wollongong, Australia, Web site: http://www.authentictasks.uow.edu.au/framework.html

Cooper, H. (1989). *Homework.* White Plains, NY: Longman.

Cooper, H. (1994). *The battle over homework.* Thousand Oaks, CA: Corwin.

Cooper, H., Robinson, J., & Patall, E. (2006). Does homework improve academic achievement? A synthesis of research, 1987–2003. *Review of Educational Research, 76,* 1–62.

Fried, R. (2005). *The game of school.* San Francisco: Jossey-Bass.

Good, T., & Brophy, J. (2008). *Looking in classrooms* (10th ed.). Boston: Pearson/Allyn & Bacon.

Kohn, A. (2006). *The homework myth.* Cambridge, MA: Da Capo Press.

Kralovec, E., & Buell, J. (2000). *The end of homework.* Boston: Beacon Press.

Marzano, R., & Pickering, D. (2007a). Errors and allegations about research on homework. *Phi Delta Kappan, 88,* 507–513.

Marzano, R., & Pickering, D. (2007b). Special topic/The case for and against homework. *Educational Leadership, 64*(6), 74–79.

Newmann, F. (1996). *Authentic achievement: Restructuring schools for intellectual quality.* San Francisco: Jossey-Bass.

Newmann, F., Marks, H., & Gamoran, A. (1996). Authentic pedagogy and student performance. *American Journal of Education, 104,* 280–312.

Renzulli, J., Gentry, M., & Reis, S. (2004). A time and a place for authentic learning. *Educational Leadership, 62,* 73–77.

Rule, A. (2006). The components of authentic learning. *Journal of Authentic Learning, 3*(1), 1–10.

Trautwein, U., Ludtke, O., Kastens, C., & Koller, O. (2006). Effort on homework in Grades 5–9: Development, motivational antecedents, and the association with effort on classwork. *Child Development, 77,* 1094–1111.

Wallis, C. (2006, August 29). The myth about homework. *Time.* Retrieved December 30, 2009, from http://www.time.com/time/magazine/article/0,9171,1376208-1,00.html

4

How Does Changing Homework Impact Your Practice?

The intent of this chapter is to give the reader an inside look at how four classroom teachers who had the all-too-familiar litany of homework frustrations assumed the role of reflectors and problem solvers. These examples demonstrate ways in which teachers can respond to the challenges and frustrations that often accompany homework. As these stories suggest, you can control the types of assignments you give and thus have the power to ameliorate many of the challenges that homework engenders.

BARBARA KNIGHTON (LOWER ELEMENTARY)

"How can I make homework meaningful to first graders?"

When I was assigned to first grade, I had to completely change my thinking, expectations, and paradigms about teaching and learning. One area in particular was home assignments. This topic was already frustrating, but now it seemed even more insurmountable.

In my previous teaching positions, I was expected to give homework assignments nightly. I often found myself fussing at children for not returning their work and trying to find time in our already overscheduled day to complete unfinished assignments. It seemed like I was becoming the "homework witch." I didn't want students to get into the habit of not completing homework, but many of my colleagues exhibited an "oh, well" attitude when it came to getting students to turn in all the assignments. I often felt like I was the only one trying to make sure that my students followed through on the assignments I gave. I tried all kinds of strategies, including having students miss recess to complete the work and having parents sign a daily assignment book. One morning, I answered a parent phone call and received some astonishing news. One of my students had flushed her homework paper down the toilet in a desperate attempt to avoid doing the work. I began to question the type and amount of work I was sending home. "How much homework is reasonable? How do I get students to return it?"

I expected parents and family members to review and check completed work for accuracy and encourage students to remember to return the assignments. Unfortunately, I found that only a few parents actually checked with their children about homework. Most often, "checking in" meant asking if they had homework and if it was done. This became embarrassingly clear during a parent-teacher conference when I shared a homework assignment turned in the previous week. Students were asked to look for any type of graph in a magazine or newspaper. Then, they were to discuss the graph and the information from it with the class. This particular student found her graph in one of her mother's *Cosmopolitan* magazines, and it certainly wasn't suitable for sharing with first graders. The mother's response was a very casual, "She found a graph, didn't she?" It was then that I began to ask, "How can I get my students' families more involved?"

My list of homework questions seemed to grow. I believe that a big part of our job is teaching students how to be learners and thinkers. In regard to homework, first-grade teachers influence habits that include completion, effort, attitude, family participation, and more. I began to see that a casual attitude about homework by the teacher could have implications for my students' future in school as well as affect expectations for class work.

I decided to create homework assignments that would help *build those important habits.* In addition to the skills-building homework required by our district math program, I began sending home family projects. My two big goals were 100 percent participation by students and appropriate family involvement. The projects were simple and accessible to all students and families. These homework assignments began shortly after school started and eventually were given once a month. The first assignment always matched our class name and helped encourage our classroom community building.

For example, one class (named the Fabulous Farm Family) decorated an outline of a scarecrow using materials found around their homes. To promote the idea of including everyone in the project, each family member signed her or his name to the finished product. Then, at school, each child would share the contributions of each person. The scarecrows decorated our classroom, connecting home to school, as well as creating a visible reminder of our shared identity.

To start this and every similar project, I would begin by modeling what was expected from the assignment. We even practiced how they might talk to their family members and invite them to help, as well as making specific plans about when and how to complete the homework. I found that the more we talked about the homework and planned together, the more confident my first graders were about their ability to succeed.

Each time, I would participate in the homework right along with my students. My patient husband would help me finish the assignment as my students were working at home on theirs. The next day, my homework was the first one shared as I modeled how to present my work to the class. Eventually, my students would begin to talk knowledgeably about Mrs. Knighton's possible contribution based on past assignments. By completing the homework myself and including my family, I showed my students how much I valued the assignment and how important it is to find the time to get it done.

As the student assignments came to school, I would celebrate and acknowledge the efforts of the student and family, thus encouraging all students to return the homework.

(Continued)

(Continued)

We would discuss the work, showing the students how important their contributions were to the project. I thanked them each and every time for helping our class by returning the homework. Families began to look forward to the next assignment and would even begin to ask for more. By my acknowledging their work, celebrating each assignment, participating myself, and including families, every homework project was completed by 90–100 percent of the students every time.

I soon began to see, however, that even though the completion percentage was high and families were participating, the academic piece was missing. I realized these homework assignments were add-ons that did not necessarily connect to the curriculum. I eventually added a writing piece (students were required to write sentences about their project), but this still wasn't truly part of the curriculum.

Sometime later, I was invited to participate in a social studies research project with professors Jere Brophy and Janet Alleman. As part of the initiative, I was asked to pilot-test a series of social studies units focusing on cultural universals. Each of the lessons included a home-to-school activity that focused on the goals and expanded/applied what was learned in school to the out-of-school activity. I noticed right away that these homework assignments were very different from the ones that I had been giving. These assignments were focused on big ideas and enhanced the lessons I was teaching. The assignments were used in many ways: as a response after a lesson, as a way to gather more information, and even to foreshadow upcoming learning. The homework was a way for me to assess my students' learning and communicate to families the content we were learning as well. So while I was able to continue using effective strategies, modeling, teacher participation, family involvement, celebrating, and using the homework in class, these extended assignments helped my students to solidify their understanding of the big ideas that I was teaching in class.

For example, during a clothing unit, students were asked to go on a "closet hunt" where they looked at tags to find specific fibers after lessons about cotton, silk, and other materials. Students had to synthesize information from several recent lessons, using reading and writing skills as well as some math skills. They were excited and motivated after I shared the contents of my closet. When students brought their homework assignments back to school, it was clear that they had spent time talking with their families about our class lesson and had used the information they had learned to finish the work. We also had a nice block of authentic data to use in class to continue our learning. We analyzed data according to fabric types and discussed fabric popularity according to season. Now, I'm using those same strategies from the social studies assignments in math, science, and health as well.

During the time I was engaged in this research and beginning to find ways of expanding my practice, I was reading books by William Glasser and Alfie Kohn. I was also able to see both men talk in person. In particular, I remember Glasser stating emphatically, "Homework should be work that must be done at home. It cannot be completed at school." I try to keep that in mind as I plan for my homework assignments. After reading Kohn's book *Punished by Rewards* (1999), I also reaffirmed celebrating and using homework assignments as a way to motivate students without extrinsic rewards like stickers or prizes.

Overall, my homework is much more authentic, meaningful, and tied to real-life experiences. My students and their families continue to participate in high numbers and enjoy the assignments as well. I've created a set of principles that I use to design and assess the assignments that I give students. Most of all, I've gotten into the habit of thinking about and analyzing my homework assignments to make sure that they are meaningful and memorable.

Jan's Follow-up to Barbara's Story

Barbara's frustration associated with a poor homework return rate by first graders is not unusual, and to some extent, her colleagues' frequent responses of "oh, well" were perhaps a bit comforting. Yet in her head and heart she was dissatisfied. Her mind-set regarding the importance of first grade for skill building and developing positive habits couldn't be erased. She was puzzled by parental apathy and lack of attentiveness to homework matters. Success for all has always been her goal, and she simply could not settle for less.

Gradually she struck upon the idea of giving homework that engaged family members in nonthreatening ways, fostered socialization, and resulted in products that could be returned to school and added to the atmosphere of the classroom. She remained a bit uneasy because even though participation was high among families, the academic piece was missing.

A real turning point came for her when she accepted the opportunity to collaborate with college professors at a nearby university. Her values meshed well with the project, and she realized that connecting the homework to unit goals and big ideas satisfied the missing link. The meaningful home assignments served to solidify students' understanding of the material, with the added bonus of giving children the opportunity to apply what they were learning.

ROB LEY (UPPER ELEMENTARY)

Before I begin each school year, I make visits to my students' homes. It sometimes takes a lot of persistence to connect. My hope is to build a classroom community that is based on meaningful relationships and respect through genuine collaboration with my students and their families. During one visit, a student's mother explained to me that all of her child's previous teachers had a special focus or interest in their teaching and that she wondered what my "thing" in teaching was. She gave examples about how her child's second-grade teacher had been most interested in teaching reading skills and how his third-grade teacher had been really good for him because she had a passion for math.

She wanted to know what I was all about. I realized how important this question was and that my response was not as simple as recalling which subject I enjoyed teaching the most. I asked myself the following questions: When are my students the most invested in their learning? What role do students' families play in making my philosophy of education become a reality? In what ways do I implement the curriculum to be respectful of young people as individual learners while still meeting curricular expectations?

I was passionate and idealistic when I started teaching. I had a fresh and unaltered perspective that my students' experience in school should be challenging, active, and relevant to their lives. Even though I was just beginning my journey in understanding how to make that vision a reality, I set high expectations for myself to achieve it. Soon after my career started, I began working with a population of at-risk students, and my stance on connecting school to real life was challenged in many ways. Looking back, I realize now that I allowed those teaching challenges to prevent me from implementing meaningful homework and ultimately expanding the curriculum to learning opportunities outside of school. I was trying to make sure that I "covered" the required material by using homework as a reinforcement of

(Continued)

(Continued)

prescribed learning materials like math sheets and fill-in-the-blank timelines. My students dedicated most of their effort to remembering and listing isolated pieces of information, rather than thinking critically about how the information could help them better understand their lives or solve important problems. These models of homework rarely reflected the backgrounds of my students' family relationships, their imagination, or their emotional position.

I also fell into the rut of allowing a generic curriculum to dictate the course of our studies. I lacked an understanding of how a shift in power relations between my students and me could make homework more meaningful. I lacked the artistry to find connections between the curriculum and my students' interests, their lives, and also the teacher-student relationship. The web of curricular interactions was limited and artificial. My students and I had formed an unspoken agreement that was based on students following my lead as long as I didn't push them to think too hard.

My educational values eventually collided with my frustrations about not meeting my own expectations in engaging students in a form of learning that was intrinsically rewarding to them. I knew that I needed to develop learning around a different curriculum framework. I wanted to maximize the number of opportunities that my students had to apply information to their lives and connect with contemporary issues. I believed that homework could be a valuable tool in creating a personal frame for my students to organize their world and share their learning with others in unique and unforgettable ways. I was at a critical place in my career when I needed to remember why I became a teacher in the first place.

Graduate school allowed me to structure my goals as a teacher, scholar, and researcher. I worked with professors on various action research projects to gain deeper insight into first understanding robust terms such as *authenticity*, *inquiry*, and *real world*. I then learned how to apply those ideas to a curriculum that is staged and often void of real-world learning. During my research, I came across other teachers who went through similar struggles relating to the challenges facing teachers who want to enrich the curriculum by making it more personally relevant to students. Steven Levy, a Walt Disney Teacher of the Year Award winner, raised a key point when he said,

> The entire world, it seems, has been rigorously processed and packaged for student consumption.
>
> Organizing learning in this way may be an effective means of teaching disassociated facts, but does it help our students understand the world? Does it prepare them to enter it as adults who have a passion for learning? Will teaching unrelated facts inspire our children to seek meaning throughout their lives? Will they learn how to solve problems or how to work with others?
>
> Compartmentalized learning does not correspond to the way human beings experience life. It robs children of the opportunity to construct for themselves categories that give their observations personal relevance and meaning (Levy, 1996, p. 19).

As educators, we cannot always alter the difficult baggage that students bring from home, but we can find ways to maximize their learning interests by carefully planning homework assignments that support unit objectives. I have realized that to accomplish this change, I had to accept that real-world problems are messy and uncertain and involve a higher level of risk taking.

My experiences with homework as an elementary student serve as a reminder that teachers can create homework that makes a difference. When I force myself to confront the pain, aggravation, and feeling of wasted time that often defined my homework experience as a student, I am motivated to make the planning of meaningful homework a daily priority and a professional responsibility. Every teacher can remember some homework assignment that inspired him or her to succeed academically. For me, it was an assignment that involved me interviewing a grocery store worker in the frozen food department about his knowledge of air currents. I remember feeling like I was participating in an exciting activity in which the results were not predetermined. The assignment was alive, and I had a sense of unsteadiness, which upon completing the assignment led to a new sense of empowerment. I believe that teachers need to reconnect to the meaningful experiences that they had as students in order to understand the learning possibilities that homework can have.

Unexpected and powerful moments have occurred when my students extended the value of learning beyond school and found their own ways of bringing the real world into the classroom. While my class was learning about our state's industries and economy, students were presented with the question "Which new industries have the best chance of stimulating Michigan's economy?" This question created a context for students to learn about both the historical background of what had driven Michigan's economy in the past and the economic concepts and issues that would entice new industries to come to Michigan in the future. I arranged for students to investigate this issue further by inviting local community members who represented different Michigan industries to the school to be interviewed by the students. After their interviews, students collectively felt that "green" industries had the best chance of becoming a new driving force in the state's economy. This led to an additional investigation into which sector of green industries should be targeted. Students interviewed a professor from Michigan State University who recently had spoken to the president of the United States about alternative fuels. He described his methods for researching cellulose ethanol and developed students' understanding of how "grassoline" could be a viable solution, strengthening our state's economy while also increasing the security of our country.

On my way to school the next morning, I saw one of my students using this knowledge! I pulled up to a stoplight and peered across the street to see Joey standing in a gas station parking lot next to a semi truck. I watched as he spoke passionately, motioning with his hands while gazing up at the bearded trucker who was hanging halfway out of his window. Joey was holding a clipboard and writing feverishly as he recorded responses from the driver about his fuel usage along with his impressions of our state's road conditions. The parent of my student later explained that her child had bombarded her with questions about the role that transportation played in our state's economy and she had agreed to let him conduct his interview that morning. The student later used his collected data and experience to present the rest of the class with the question "Who should be responsible for paying for the improvement of our roads?"

The creation of problem-solving during this unit continued to create a meaningful context for homework as my students explored questions related to geography and economics. For example, a student's relative flying into Detroit needed to arrive in our town—150 miles away—by that evening. Given that the student's parents were not able to pick up the relative at the airport, the questions became "How could the relative get to the local site in a timely manner?" and "What are the costs and trade-offs associated with each form of

(Continued)

(Continued)

transport?" Although I had presented the assignment as optional, students took it very seriously, with most of them engaging family members in figuring out what to do. Students reported various proposed solutions after calls to Greyhound, Amtrak, travel agencies, etc. One student had had a long conversation with a limousine service, going so far as negotiating a better price than the original quote.

I have learned that sometimes the most important learning opportunities are right before our eyes, but because they are not considered "real school," we pass them up in favor of the prescriptive and incredibly organized pedagogy that characterizes "official" learning. To understand the need for more meaningful homework to be pumped into our normal curricular endeavors, I have considered the differences between how learning takes place in the classroom versus outside of formal school situations. I have come to the conclusion that these prescribed "learning experiences" need to be balanced with learning that is characterized by student interest, that is instantaneously relevant, and that motivates students to produce something that holds high importance to them.

Teachers need to make decisions about homework that reflect their beliefs about the ways in which young people learn best. Small changes in homework assignments and added communication with parents can make a huge difference in the way that students perceive the meaningfulness of an assignment. They also can strengthen the role that students play in the direction and depth of a unit of study.

Jan's Follow-up to Rob's Story

Rob's challenges as a novice teacher began to mask his true beliefs, and the passion and idealism he brought to teaching started to disappear. He believed that students' learning opportunities should be challenging, active, and relevant to their lives, but he felt overwhelmed. As a result, the generic curriculum gradually became the norm.

Because reflection was a big part of his teacher education program, Rob was uneasy about his current practice. The parent's question "What was he about?" really hit home. His education values were colliding with his frustrations! His timing in returning to graduate school could not have been better. Authenticity, inquiry, and the real world were talked about often, and then one day as he was poring over his assignments, he read Levy's quote: "The entire world seems to have been rigorously processed and packaged for student consumption" (1996, p. 19). He was compelled to shift gears.

Rob rethought his own experiences as an elementary school student and began to replay one of his most memorable assignments: the out-of-school activity of gathering data at the grocery store. That memory had him spinning. It confirmed the power of inquiry and the idea that homework could be motivating.

Cleverly, he began bringing real learning into the classroom by posing questions that connected the known and closely aligned to standards (e.g., history of the state's economy) to queries with unknown answers, such as "What could drive the state's economy in the future?" The results were amazing. Kids had a stake in the content, which addressed what was required but sailed beyond that benchmark at record rates. Gradually he cast a broader net and found students and parents taking the questions he posed far beyond his wildest expectations.

Sharing power with students and unleashing their ideas, which went far beyond the prescribed learning experiences, sold Rob on the importance of meaningful home assignments. His work became easier and far more interesting. His passion returned!

SARAH MIDDLESTEAD (MIDDLE SCHOOL)

For the first years of my teaching career, Monday was much like Tuesday, which was much like the rest of the week. Though the days changed, the routine was painfully the same. I would introduce a skill, give examples, and then assign 15 to 25 problems directly from our textbook. Students would be given time to start the assignment during class and then expected to finish the remainder at home, as homework. That was it. Homework was always assigned from the textbook and given on most days. A typical day of class would begin with me asking if there were any questions about last night's homework assignment. My middle school mathematics students would look blankly at me and then their textbook, trying to remember what last night's homework assignment even was. Eventually, their eyes would register a dim recognition as a sheet of half-finished problems was pulled from the depths of their math textbooks. Though students clearly had not touched the paper since they'd left math class the day before, no questions would be asked. They were staring at incomplete homework, but no one would raise a hand to ask for guidance, clarification, or assistance with the many unfinished problems. It was a showdown of sorts, me desperately wanting, and waiting for, some kind soul to put me out of my misery by asking me to guide the class through a problem, and the students patiently waiting for me to get over the illusion that a question would actually be asked. That was the start of every single class period. It was painful—for all of us.

I am, however, remiss in saying that students never asked questions. There were some questions that were asked with such fervor and frequency that I soon began to dread them: "Why do we have to do this?" and "When will I ever use this?" What I dreaded even more than these questions were the answers that soon began to flow from my mouth in an effort to quell the unrest of the masses: "Because you will need it someday," and "Actually, you might not ever use this."

After years of this daily routine, I began to seriously question how homework was being used in my classroom. Homework was, in fact, a topic of great distress to me. In the first five years of my teaching career, I had countless students who received a grade lower than that of which they were capable simply because they did not complete homework assignments. Students could perform well on assessments, but because they did not turn in homework, their class grades were significantly lower. At first, I thought it was simply that my students were not motivated; they were lazy. It was not my fault if they did not take homework assignments seriously. After all, I presented lessons to them that were thoughtfully designed, carefully aligned to both state and national benchmarks. What students did with the information I gave them was completely up to them and beyond my control.

I could not explain the homework phenomena that were occurring in my classroom. Some students would do no homework but still pass tests. At the same time, I would watch in bewilderment as students who *did* do homework *failed* the tests. What I was witnessing did not make sense; students could do the homework and fail, not do the homework and pass. I saw every scenario in between. Clearly, homework, as I was using it, was not having a positive impact on learning.

In addition to the homework completion and test score discrepancies I was seeing, I felt that other factors were at work in this homework battle. For example, one year I had two classes comprised of students of very low socioeconomic status with past histories of discipline problems and truancy. I knew that it would be virtually impossible for students to complete homework, due to challenges in their lives outside of school, so I simply did not assign it in these two classes. We did all of our work in class. Conversely, my other two classes were comprised of students of higher socioeconomic status. These students had

(Continued)

(Continued)

better homework completion rates, so I kept up with the practice of assigning homework. In every class, the same unit tests were given. What I found was astonishing: all four classes performed virtually the same on the unit tests. Doing homework or not doing it seemed to make no difference.

Based on what I was observing, the use of homework did not seem to be an accurate predictor of academic achievement. This forced me to address both the ways and types of homework I was using. I could no longer attribute homework struggles to a lack of motivation or plain old laziness. There was something bigger going on, and I was determined to find out what it was.

Fueled by my graduate studies, I decided to launch a research project to see what would happen if I changed the nature of homework assignments. I began by reading authors such as Harris Cooper, Alfie Kohn, Robert Marzano, and Fred Newmann. It was critical to me that any changes I made in my classroom were based on solid research. What I found in my reading made a significant impact on my teaching. I was forced to look deeply at my own practice to evaluate how I was using homework, which was quite a humbling experience. The literature suggested that appropriate homework can increase student achievement; however, I was not seeing this in my classroom. I decided that the key must be in this idea of *appropriate homework*. That was it! What was the nature of the homework tasks I was assigning? For me, *appropriate homework* was going to be *meaningful homework*. I wanted homework assignments, the basis of which would be data collection and interviews, to be an enhancement of the curriculum, a chance to extend knowledge to the world outside the school walls.

The literature I read revolutionized my thinking, leaving an imprint on my mind that could not be erased. For example, I had always seen inequalities among students. I knew that students who were economically disadvantaged were just that—disadvantaged—but I'd never realized how deeply those disadvantages reached. Poor students have so much stacked against them. They do not have access to materials needed to complete homework and rarely have the parental support needed to be academically successful. The most profound thing I learned from my reading was just how grievously and unfairly homework impacts disadvantaged students. Until reading authors such as Alfie Kohn, Etta Kralovec, and John Buell, I assigned homework without thinking twice. I did not think about whether my students had equal access to the materials needed to complete the tasks. I rarely thought about the impact that a homework assignment might have on a student living in poverty.

I had become impassioned in my belief that homework was not accessible to all students. So I started to design new kinds of homework. For my first attempt at the design and use of meaningful homework, students were asked to interview someone at home about his or her own personal "math history," what his or her experiences had been with mathematics. I felt that this assignment had equal accessibility for all students regardless of their economic level. By this I mean that all students would be able to find someone to interview (a parent, sibling, grandparent, neighbor, teacher, etc.). I was astonished at what I saw! This interview was completed with much higher rates than any assignment I had given from the textbook. In addition, the results fueled classroom discussion about math and how the people in our lives use it. I found that through this interview, students gained new insight into mathematics and it usefulness in the world, which in turn increased their desire to learn more about mathematics. This experience encouraged me to delve further into the idea of meaningful homework.

After changing the nature of my homework tasks, I rarely had to answer the questions "Why do we have to do this?" and "When will I ever use this?" Through the use of authentic homework, these questions are answered. Students began to see how math is used in the world because their homework was designed to intentionally link classroom learning with how the world works. In fact, I find that if I am hit with a barrage of "Why do we have to do this?" and "When will I ever use this?" questions, I have not done my job. I have not explicitly embedded into students' learning—specifically, their homework assignments—a real-world context for mathematics.

Am I perfect at this? Absolutely and painfully not! (I believe that my students would agree.) Questions about homework still come much more quickly than answers. I have, however, begun my journey to make homework authentic and accessible to all of my students. Nothing has impacted my growth as a professional like this change! I have come to realize that I have more control over homework than I once thought. Whether students actually do their homework is still out of my hands, but we, as teachers, can structure homework so that students actually want to do it. A middle school student who wants to do homework? Impossible, you say! I have seen it happen, and I have seen the resulting increase in student achievement and self-efficacy.

Jan's Follow-up to Sarah's Story

Taking graduate courses, coupled with Sarah's curiosity about finding answers to nagging questions associated with her practice, saved her from falling into the trap of just "doing teaching." While she was dutifully following school policies associated with homework, she began to realize that her assignments—and her students' responses to them—were not accurate predications of academic achievement.

Reading what the authorities had to say about homework led to some eye-opening questions for her: How am I using homework? Is it appropriate? How can it be made more so? Gradually the meaning of *appropriate* shifted to *authentic*.

Given Sarah's sensitivity to her students, she couldn't help but think about their access to resources—a secret to success for those in her community. She began to pilot-test activities that were authentic and made sense for her as well as her students. The ultimate rewards came when those middle schoolers were no longer asking, "Why do we have to do this?" Instead, they were enthusiastic about their homework and were anxious to share the real-life connections offered by the content.

BEN BOTWINSKI (HIGH SCHOOL)

Mr. Hines: Coach, can I have a minute? My name is Joel Hines. My son is Sean.

Coach: Sure, Mr. Hines. What's on your mind?

Mr. Hines: Well, as you know, I have been coming down to watch you guys practice for a couple of weeks now, and it seems to me that Sean isn't getting a good look at linebacker.

(Continued)

(Continued)

Coach: Well, Mr. Hines, let me reassure you that he is getting just as much of an opportunity as every other player on our team. Our coaching staff knows that Sean is a hard worker, and he is certainly in the hunt for a linebacker position. Allow me to reassure you that I have no hidden agenda, Mr. Hines. I am only interested in putting the best 11 players I can find on the field.

The most remarkable aspect of this brief conversation with Mr. Hines was its eventual impact on my teaching. Less than a week later, on the first day of school, Sean Hines walked into my classroom surrounded by a small entourage of friends and admirers. I made it a point to walk over and formally introduce myself to Sean and the other students. We joked and made small talk. I answered a few questions and then moved on to the next group of students. My third year of teaching and coaching had begun.

Weeks passed, and while the team struggled, I felt as though my teaching was finally gaining momentum. My freshman students were reading and writing about influential political philosophers, and they were drawing connections between the works of those philosophers and the subsequent shape of the Declaration of Independence and the U.S. Constitution. The majority of my students were contributing meaningfully to classroom discourse and debate. I was pleased! Certainly the situation wasn't perfect; homework completion rates were low. But I simply dismissed it as laziness or lack of motivation on the part of my students. In my mind, I was doing everything I could to be a first-rate teacher.

Like so many other professional educators, I was spending hours designing lessons and homework assignments that I believed were both meaningful and interesting. No worksheets. No "chapter review" questions. All of the work in my classroom was reading and writing based. The students were required to take some notes, but the vast majority of time was spent reading and discussing short passages from primary source documents such as speeches, essays, and music lyrics. We would even occasionally analyze photographs and political cartoons. Homework was no different. Students were often required to read and analyze an abbreviated passage from a primary source. Sometimes they were asked to take a particular stance on an issue of historical significance. Other times, they were asked to comment on a particular excerpt. Assignments were typically accompanied by a detailed explanation of my expectations, and "final products" were usually modeled prior to the due date.

Mr. Scott: Coach, can I have a minute?

Coach: Sure, Mr. Scott What's on your mind?

Mr. Scott: Well, it has been brought to my attention that nearly twenty percent of the students enrolled in your class are failing. And as your building principal, I'm concerned!

Coach: I can explain, Mr. Scott. Many of the students who are struggling are not completing their work, particularly their homework assignments. As a result, those students are in danger of failing the marking period. I have made an attempt to contact parents via e-mail and progress reports, but only a handful have responded at this point. I intend to begin making phone calls later this week.

Mr. Scott: Are you assigning a lot of homework?

Coach: Weekly assignments, sir, though the work is rigorous. It requires students to read, analyze, and write—tasks many students are not fond of completing outside of school.

Mr. Scott: All right, keep me posted. I am not sure if we are going to be able to offer summer school for social studies, and we certainly can't have thirty students failing your class.

―――――

This was not my first professional conversation of this nature, or even my second. At the end of the previous academic year, Mr. Boyd (the school counselor in charge of mailing summer school notifications) stopped me in the hall and asked why so many students were likely to be enrolled in a social studies section over the summer. As an untenured teacher, sometimes it was unclear exactly to whom I was accountable. So I explained that it was important to me to maintain a high degree of academic rigor. I stated that I refused to compromise my expectations simply because students were unwilling to work to their full potential. While that answer seemed to pacify Mr. Boyd, our conversation shook the fragile foundation on which I had been constructing my teaching identity. Subsequent discussions with my mentor teacher, the building principal, and the school counselor provided little reassurance.

Call it youthful naiveté, ignorant optimism, or even old-fashioned arrogance, but I believed that good teachers maintained high expectations for both themselves and their students. They challenged their students to complete the type of work that they—the students— would not otherwise have believed possible. I also understood that when it came to the classroom, it was important that students be provided the necessary background information and support to be successful. Yet the senior members of my professional teaching community seemed to be implicitly suggesting otherwise. None of them directly recommended that I lower my expectations or decrease the academic rigor, but the fact that 20 percent of my social studies students were flirting with failure was clearly not going to be tolerated.

The truth of the matter is that homework was, for me, a constant source of frustration and disappointment. Despite performing well on in-class activities and assessments, many students refused to complete the assigned homework and thus were perpetually struggling to pass my class. But how was I to amend the situation without lowering my expectations or compromising my standards? What else could I do to remedy the homework challenge? Nobody, not my building principal, the counselor, or my mentor teacher, offered any advice. In fact, I had often overheard more experienced and respected teachers lamenting similar challenges, so I felt powerless over the situation. In what can only be described as a "teaching defense mechanism," I eventually gave up and dismissed the homework situation as the students' problem, choosing instead to direct my energies and efforts into areas where I believed I had some control.

―――――

Sean: Coach, can I have minute?

Coach: Sure, Sean. What's on your mind?

Sean: I saw that you left another message on our answering machine. You know my dad is not going to call you back.

Coach: Well, it is important that I speak with him, Sean. You are not completing your social studies homework, and I would like to talk to him directly.

Sean: He knows that I am struggling, but as long as I am doing well enough to continue playing ball, he is not going to get that upset.

(Continued)

(Continued)

Coach: Sean, you are dangerously close to not meeting minimum eligibility standards. Furthermore, if you have any desire to continue playing football after high school, you are going to have to work harder in the classroom.

Sean: I know, Coach. I know that I need to work harder. My dad is going to be at our game this evening; maybe you could talk to him then.

Coach: That's a good idea, Sean. I will try talking to him before the game. Now please get to class.

———

Mr. Hines wasn't able to attend our game that evening, nor was he able to return any of my subsequent phone calls. And even though Sean's work habits did marginally improve, the entire scenario left me irritated. I knew Sean's father was a single parent raising three school-age children. I knew he cared deeply about his son, but I honestly questioned his perception of the value of education! That is, until he knocked on the door of my classroom one late October morning. After entering the room and exchanging a handshake with me, Mr. Hines apologized for not returning my calls. He explained that since Sean had entered high school, he was struggling to relate to his eldest son. Mr. Hines expressed frustration with regard to his perceived lack of ability to assist with homework, and he revealed his own high school pains and disappointments. Our meeting adjourned with a second handshake and a mutual promise to do everything we could to help Sean succeed.

The story of Sean and Mr. Hines highlights the relationship that exists between parental involvement and homework completion. As a result of the experience described above, I recognized that I was grappling with two distinct challenges: the immediate challenge of increasing homework completion rates without compromising my standards and a broader challenge related to parental involvement (or the lack thereof). If these challenges were related, then in what ways? What aspects of my classroom routines, teaching practice, homework design, and homework policy were contributing to these challenges? Furthermore, how could I minimize the presence of these difficulties? What factors were within my direct control as a classroom teacher? If could find answers to these questions, I felt I would be well on my way to making positive changes. But where was I to look for answers?

After being challenged by a professor in one of my graduate teaching courses to begin thinking deeply about the role of the teacher in the homework process, I recognized that the answer—at least for me—was personal and involved professional introspection. It was during this time that I came to understand that while quiet contemplation certainly is important and has its place, many people intuitively understand that learning is a social endeavor. I realized that homework should be no different. When I recognized that I could make small adjustments to many of my existing homework assignments that would both enhance communication with parents and make homework more meaningful, I had to give it a try. I began tinkering toward meaningfulness by revising those assignments that I perceived to be less meaningful. I also created mini assignments (more authentic in nature), which were then "coupled" with my existing homework. My early attempts at meaningfulness were directed towards the incorporation of adults into the learning process (largely through informal interviews) in interesting and responsible ways. The results were immediately noticeable, and those early successes prompted further exploration of the power of meaningful homework.

Jan's Follow-up to Ben's Story

Ben, not atypical of many almost-tenured teachers, thought he was doing everything he could to be an effective teacher. After all, he had introduced a lot of academic rigor into his courses. The majority of students were contributing to class discussions, and homework was no longer mindless dittoes. He had been forewarned that high schoolers were a special breed, and a 20 percent failure rate because of incomplete homework did not seem unusual.

Not surprisingly, he was stunned and a little miffed when the principal questioned him about those failing students. He thought, "So what am I supposed to do about it? It's their fault." Encounters with parents added to his frustrations. Secretly he wished parents could be as geeked about academics as they were about athletics!

His struggles were perfectly timed with the requirement to do an action research project for one of his graduate classes. Once he got past the "blame game," he approached homework problems with enthusiasm. The rest is history. Through his own research, Ben became convinced that engaging families increases in-class interest/participation and provides a contemporary twist to content that is truly motivating and meaningful to both the students and the teacher.

CONCLUSION

In all the preceding narratives, the changes made by teachers were gradual and strategic. They didn't always come easily or naturally, but they resulted in tremendous payoffs. The shifts that Barb, Rob, Sarah, and Ben made in their practice occurred because of their openness and the time and effort they invested in the art of reflection. If you were to question them, they would tell you that creating meaningful homework continues to be challenging: "While we are far from having it all figured out, the synergy created with families and students around the content can be serendipitous. We'd never return to our past practices."

Chapters 5 and 6 are intended to focus on you—the teacher—and what you can do to make homework more meaningful and memorable for your students.

REFERENCES

Kohn, A. (1999). *Punished by rewards.* Boston: Houghton Mifflin.

Levy, S. (1996). *Starting from scratch: One classroom builds its own curriculum.* Portsmouth, NH: Heinemann.

Part II

Assemble the Plan

Part II is intended to focus on you—the teacher—and what you can do to make homework more meaningful and memorable for your students.

5

How Can You Design Meaningful Homework?

The purposes of this chapter are to provide you with general factors to consider in designing homework, including inquiry skills that are necessary for the successful completion of meaningful assignments, and a guide for planning your own meaningful homework assignments.

DESIGN FACTORS

Our position on homework activities has been influenced by the work of John Dewey, Hilda Taba, Ralph Tyler, and other major curricular theorists and by the research conducted by Brophy and Alleman (1991). For example, Zais (1976) stated that the primary standard for selection of learning activities should be how well the activities contribute to students' attainment of curricular goals. Other criteria for good activities are that they provide for the attainment of multiple goals, engage students in active forms of learning, help them develop values and critical-thinking capacities, are built around important content, and are well matched to students' abilities and interests.

> **Primary Principles**
>
> Goal Relevance
>
> Appropriate Level of Difficulty
>
> Feasible
>
> Cost-Effective

Primary Principles of Design

While the efforts of Brophy and Alleman are focused on social studies, the principles they developed are equally applicable to other school subjects when educators prepare instructional activities, including home assignments. These principles are as follows.

Goal Relevance

Activities must be useful as a means of accomplishing worthwhile curricular goals (i.e., goal relevance). While activities may serve many goals, each activity should have a primary goal. Activities that amount to mere busywork do not meet this criterion, nor do games or pastimes that lack a curricular purpose. Activities should be built around powerful ideas or central questions, not isolated facts or other peripheral content that lacks life-application potential.

Appropriate Level of Difficulty

Another primary principle refers to appropriate level of difficulty. The assignment must be difficult enough to provide some challenge and extend learning, but not so difficult as to leave many students confused or frustrated. Difficult new processes should not be introduced in the context of applying challenging or unfamiliar content. When the main purpose is to get students to apply new content, activities should employ easy or familiar formats and processes.

Feasible

Home assignments can use the students' total environment to provide data or learning resources. This makes certain activities feasible that might not be feasible in the classroom. For example, students might attend a school board meeting and report back to the class.

Cost-Effective

Cost-effectiveness does not need to be assigned as high a priority for home assignments as for in-class activities. Class time is limited and needs to be concentrated on lessons and structuring assignments, but once the students are clear about what they need to do, they can work on assignments out of class. They also can work on individually negotiated or time-consuming projects that complement the group lessons and activities that occur during class time. The time factor does warrant consideration, however, in planning when and how the home assignments will be used during in-class instruction to add diversity of opinions, up-to-dateness, personalization, etc.

Secondary Principles of Design

Brophy and Alleman (1991) also developed a set of secondary principles for designing and implementing learning activities. These refer to features that are desirable but not absolutely necessary. The secondary principles are as follows.

Multiple Goals

A home assignment that simultaneously accomplishes several lesson or unit goals is preferable to one that accomplishes only a single goal. Assignments that allow for integration across subjects may be desirable; however, such integration should not interfere with the accomplishment of the primary goal.

Most successful integration occurs not as a result of deliberate attempts to inject it into the curriculum but as a natural by-product of a goal-oriented attempt to provide authentic applications of big ideas, central questions, skills, formulas, etc.

Motivational Value

Other things being equal, home assignments that students enjoy are preferable to those that students do not enjoy. Typically, authentic, holistic, life-application activities not only have greater pedagogical value but are more enjoyable than information recognition or retrieval worksheets or other isolated skill practice exercises.

Like integration, motivation is important but nevertheless considered a secondary principle. Too often, curriculum developers or teachers treat it as primary by planning "fun" activities that lack goal relevance. Sometimes these are tacked on to tedious assignments or are used simply to fulfill a homework policy requirement. No matter how much students may enjoy the homework, unless it promotes progress toward some worthwhile goal, it is not considered a good assignment.

Higher-Order Thinking

The best homework activities challenge students not just to locate and reproduce information but also to interpret, analyze, or manipulate information in response to questions or problems that cannot be resolved through routine application of previously learned knowledge. Often, the necessary skills, such as questioning, interviewing, hypothesizing, or evaluating sources of information, need to be reviewed or isolated for short segments of direct instruction to ensure that students possess them and are positioned to apply them. For students to be successful with the home assignment, they need to feel comfortable applying the skills associated with it.

Adaptability

Home assignments that can be adapted to accommodate students' individual differences and abilities are preferable. Other things being equal, home assignments that include an element of choice are favored over assignments that lack this feature. The choices should all match the goals. They might refer to how to do the assignment, the number of individuals to interview or survey, the number of sources to use, the types of information to collect, etc.

Assets

Another factor to consider in designing meaningful homework is student, family, and community assets. Moll, Amanti, Neff, and Gonzalez (2001) referred to this as "funds of knowledge." This concept rests on the principle that recognition of the strengths, gifts, and talents of individuals and communities is more likely to inspire positive action than an exclusive focus on needs and problems (see Table 5.1). The goal is to end the negative cycle of self-fulfilling prophecies that derive from deficit thinking and to increase students' self-efficacy and motivation. For homework, this translates into highlighting students' interests, strengths, etc., in creating assignments. For example, if students love basketball but are uninterested in learning about angles, consider giving them a drawing of a basketball court and designing a homework task that asks them to plot the percentage of baskets made at various angles. Analyzing the data will provide the basis for a rich conversation during the next class session. There is a high degree of probability that if this approach is incorporated regularly, deficits can be overcome.

Table 5.1   Student, Family, and Community Assets

Student Assets	Family Assets	Community Assets
• Plays a musical instrument.	• Ancestry	• Community artisans
• Interested in drama.	• Location of home	• Corporations
• Excels at sports.	• Occupations of parents	• School board members
• Speaks another language.	• Experiences of grandparents	• Local industries
• Has a unique skill.	• Older or younger siblings	• Library, YMCA, parks and recreation, etc.

Student Voice and Choice

Incorporating student voice and choice can be very effective when doing so supports the overall lesson/unit goals. For example, some students may choose to write their final product, while others may choose to present it in a video format. Some might go beyond the basic requirements by surveying more people or interviewing additional subjects. Allowing students some freedom makes the assignment more personalized and therefore more meaningful.

INQUIRY SKILLS

Homework assignments become more personally relevant to students if they include inquiry skills that assist them in finding solutions to real questions and issues. An effective use of inquiry skills enables content to be brought to life while also challenging students to apply the content to authentic situations.

Inquiry skills are abilities used every day in the process of solving problems or applying new information. These skills form the basic foundation of any investigation. Following is a list of skills that we believe teachers should consider using when creating meaningful assignments:

- Ask questions
- Identify problems
- Collect and analyze data
- Make observations
- Choose sources and collect evidence
- Summarize findings and reflect

This list is not exhaustive, and most of the skills can be expanded for greater student understanding. These inquiry skills are a prominent feature of national standards, and they transcend all subjects and grade levels. They can be used as assignment organizers in the planning process or as supportive strategies that students can use to get the most out of an assignment. A discussion of each inquiry skill follows.

Ask Questions

Students who are able to ask thoughtful questions are better equipped to transfer and apply concepts taught in class to the world outside of school. Students need to be directly involved in the process of generating effective questions. A thoughtfully worded question about a situation that takes place outside of school can yield expanded investigation and interest.

Even the most reluctant students can become interested in exploring new content once they have been able to formulate questions related to their interests or concerns. A powerful question can empower students to feel like real investigators and demonstrate the open-ended nature of the content. Asking questions is also beneficial because a student-created question can be shared with a wider audience such as family members, guest speakers, community members, or students from other classrooms. A question could also receive a variety of responses based on the different perspectives of the people who answer it.

Family members can become important resources in thinking about ideas in diverse ways. When family members help students formulate questions, they also become invested in finding out the answers. Emphasizing the value of a family member's question within the classroom context can also validate the family member's credibility in the eyes of the student.

For example, a class has identified a new state law in Florida that requires schools to develop online classes for K–12 students. Students are considering the impact of such an initiative in their own district and are curious about the opinions of their families and community members. For homework, students share information about the law with others and gather their responses about replacing face-to-face school experiences with computer-based instruction. They then compile the responses to determine a set of questions that can be made into a community survey.

Teachers can also use students' questions to assess how their students are internalizing classroom and homework experiences, and the frequency with which students are asking questions can help teachers consider new ways to make the content more meaningful. If a student is asking productive questions that will further research or the planning of an investigation, then it is likely that the student believes the content is valuable.

Identify Problems

The world is filled with problems, dilemmas, and controversial issues that students can recognize, interpret, and share with others. Meaningful homework can be enhanced by the integration of problems that are anchored in content and based on real-life situations. Identifying problems that impact students' lives can drive the inquiry process. The skill of identifying problems challenges students to determine why the situation is a problem, what population it impacts, how particular situations pose difficulties, the various perspectives that exist, and potential solutions that could be adopted.

Identifying a real-world problem is different from solving problems such as the ones we usually find in math class. Real-world problems do not necessarily have existing solutions, often are messy and ill structured, and usually can be interpreted in different ways. Incorporating problems related to contemporary issues brings content to life while simultaneously infusing a greater sense of purpose to the content learning.

"Real" problems do not have to be huge social challenges such as poverty, global warming, or endangered species. Although these problems can be used effectively in the classroom, unless the connection between the problem and a student's life is clear, the student may not view the problem as relevant. Teachers and students might consider frustrations or worries that they have on a day-to-day basis or look to local problems as a source of connection to the wider world. For example, students studying immigration could identify problems that their ancestors may have faced and then compare them to problems experienced by recent immigrants. The class could research immigration in their city and then connect with a local refugee center. Petitions, letters, guest speaker interviews, and student grant writing all present opportunities for students to respond constructively to problems that they have identified.

Often problems are more easily and meaningfully discovered outside of school, as students become "problem detectives." Problems can be found in different forms of media, conversations with selected individuals, or reflections on personal or collective adversities. When students discover problems, they gain a sense of ownership that will sustain their interest longer than if the teacher had presented the problem. A problematic situation can serve as a valuable organizing center for meaningful homework assignments because it nurtures students' interests in further investigation or finding feasible solutions. When students identify problems outside of the classroom, they see, read, and analyze the world differently. Perhaps most important, they apply content in more useful ways.

Collect and Analyze Data

Although data collection is a skill that most students begin to develop at an early age, they still require support to determine what data to collect and how to collect it. The basic methods for collecting data are through interviews, surveys, and use of various media. Homework data collection can include any source that is relevant to the content being learned, whether it is the pH of a nearby lake, two public officials' views on the same event, or the percentage of grocery shoppers who use plastic rather than reusable bags. Designing assignments that challenge students to collect and analyze data provides opportunities for students to get their hands on real numbers, responses, and details that can keep the curriculum up-to-date and personalize learning. A key component of data collection is to teach students which tools and technologies will be most helpful in gathering accurate data. Homework assignments that require data collection provide teachers and students with the opportunity to foster a respect for data, interpretation, and communication skills across subject boundaries.

Collecting data as a homework assignment can require students to use tools and various forms of technology in meaningful ways. By applying these tools in a real-world context, students learn that they can provide more information than can be collected by just using their senses or "taking somebody's word for it."

Back in the classroom, teachers can underscore the importance of data with questions like these: How does your data support your idea? How do you know? Why do you think that's true? Teachers can also encourage open discussion of unexpected results and possible theories. Data collected individually can be combined to create a classroom data set. Its variance can highlight the diversity of the learning community, while its consistencies can emphasize its coherence. Furthermore, students can share the data with family or community members for homework assignments. For more advanced students, concepts such as representative sampling and selection bias can be introduced. It is also important that students understand when and how to filter more useful from less useful data. Through these data explorations, students will find themselves becoming increasingly connected to the content through the integration of different subjects and real-world problems.

Make Observations

Making observations is a special kind of data collection. As with all the skills described, teachers need to involve students in learning about the process of how to make effective use of their observation skills. Useful observations are thorough and accurate statements that can be much more than sketches or diagrams. They could include taking photographs, watching an event, or noticing changes to the community. Additionally, observations can involve students using more than their eyes. All five senses can be incorporated into homework assignments, and observations can include both qualitative and quantitative examples. One important aspect of this skill is that the students document (in whatever form is appropriate) what is taking place. They should record their observations and share their findings with the class. Teachers can help students think about purposes and goals by asking questions such as these: How is that observation important? What does this observation tell you about what we are studying? How might your observation support or refute a particular assertion?

Another important aspect of making keen observations involves understanding subtle differences. For example, a student may observe two people engaging in conversation and simply document the fact that they were talking. However, a keen observer would also note the subtleties of the conversation, such as the body language that is expressed, whether or not one person seems to be driving the conversation, etc.

Students also can investigate how their observations may change over time. For example, students recording the impact of erosion may notice a change over the course of a few weeks. After documenting the occurrence, they could begin to ask questions about their observations and share these with family and community members. Additionally, it is important for students to consider what they think they will see, what they did see, and how their observations can be explained.

Choose Sources and Collect Evidence

Meaningful homework assignments present many opportunities for students to choose sources and collect evidence to support their thinking. Teaching students to evaluate sources in an active, reflective manner enables them to consider a range of perspectives. Ultimately, students must question whether or not their source or evidence represents an accurate and fair perspective. Teachers who integrate this skill into the classroom and into their homework assignments should place a premium on finding a balanced representation of information. Students learn to evaluate whether or not a source is biased by considering factors such as gender, race, age, life experiences, profession, and geographic region.

Additionally, students need to learn to evaluate the balance of the informational sources being used. They should work toward gathering a diverse selection of information from many different people and media (e.g., Internet resources, photographs, songs, television programming, and advertisements). Students can be taught to choose sources thoughtfully, using a critical lens to evaluate the patterns that may emerge from their conversations, data, or observations. Through the practice of evaluating sources, students come to realize that meaning is not constant across diverse perspectives.

Examining the challenges associated with collecting and using each source deepens and expands the application of the skill. For example, when using the Internet, students should take precautions to make sure that the information is reliable. When using people and their opinions or ideas as evidence, students should focus on determining which combination of perspectives will give them the most comprehensive results. Convenience often becomes the default factor in selecting sources, so providing sufficient time to choose and collect information can greatly strengthen application of the skill.

This skill also offers students the opportunity to critique the values and voices that are shared within the classroom. Students' diversity and range of opinions can be used as strengths in understanding different facets of complex issues and topics. By using this skill outside of school while considering multiple perspectives, students become active participants in their community and make connections with others through the information they learn.

Summarize Findings and Reflect

Reflection and summarization activities can help students increase awareness of their learning. Summarizing findings and reflecting give students the chance to make important connections between their work outside of the classroom and their work in the classroom. Moreover, reflection activities such as project logs and journals provide opportunities for students to share progress and concerns on an ongoing basis. Homework effectiveness and student learning can both be enhanced when teachers review student reflections and then provide appropriate feedback and guidance.

It is important to help students understand how their conclusions can change depending on the evidence presented. Observations and other data may need to be elaborated. Students can benefit from being given the time to justify the reasons for their findings and the opportunity to change their original thinking based on introduction of additional evidence.

For example, students could use this skill when studying issues related to Native American history and the Native person's experience in America during the past and in modern times. As a preassessment at the start of the unit, each student could draw an image of a Native person, and then the class could discuss why many of the images were similar and contained tipis, war weapons, or chiefs. They then could search their households and gather images and other sources depicting Native American people in different forms, such as logos, advertisements, phrases, cartoons, toys, food containers, books, photographs, and movies. They also could discuss with a family member questions such as these: Are we more likely to encounter a stereo-typed image of a Native American or meet a real, flesh-and-blood Native person? Should athletic team names with Native American connotations be accepted and celebrated? Should we use the word *Indian* or *Native American*? Students then could present to the class the artifacts from home and summarize their thoughts about the impact that Native American stereotypes could have on their unit of study. They also could reflect on how their understandings have shifted to include a more diverse and current consideration of Native cultures; then they could share their summaries and reflections with a guest speaker, who could talk in more detail about modern issues impacting local Native cultures.

Summarizing findings and reflections is an important tool to ensure successful homework assignments. Findings and reflections provide a means through which students can make sense of what they are seeing and doing and learn from it. The reflection process is essentially never ending and assists them in probing through basic questions like *what? so what?* and *now what?* Without a commitment to deliberate and guided reflection, students may not learn much from their experiences. Reflection leads to understanding, which in turn leads to more informed action and further inquiry.

Questions for Promoting Inquiry Skills

Who in our community could students interview about this topic?

How could students' questions about this topic be addressed and expanded?

Which issues connected to this topic does our community grapple with?

What information about this topic could students collect or count?

Does this topic have controversial aspects that might heighten students' interest or commitment?

What differing views about this topic might exist in our community?

In what ways could students use their findings to influence an intended audience?

Inquiry skills help to establish shared expectations, a common vocabulary, and increased accessibility for all students. When students know how to use these skills in and outside of school, they can focus their energies on accomplishing the task at hand rather than trying to figure out the process that needs to be followed to meet expectations.

Teaching Inquiry Skills in the Classroom

One possible scenario for teaching inquiry skills in the classroom involves a "skills workshop." Teachers can create a time and place for these skills to be emphasized through direct teaching, teacher modeling, opportunities for practice, and chances to apply the skill to a new learning experience on their own.

A skills workshop lesson can take as little as 10 minutes and should be viewed as an embedded routine within the everyday classroom structure. To improve the likelihood of student success, the teacher should teach new skills with familiar content in the workshop so that students are able to focus on the skill and the manner in which it is used. Table 5.2 outlines one format for a skills workshop lesson.

Table 5.2 Skills Workshop Lesson Steps

1. **Create a purpose, describe, and connect.**	Emphasize a need for using the skill. Explain the kind of results that the skill can help generate. Display varying levels of skill proficiency. Link the skill to students' prior experiences with other skills, content, and their lives.
2. **Demonstrate and think out loud.**	Verbalize your thinking while showing your students the skill in action. Explain how the skill can be used to organize ideas and information while analyzing its effectiveness and the challenges you encounter.
3. **Try it together.**	Provide students with an opportunity to practice the skill with a partner, a small group, or the whole class. Give guided practice and involve students who may struggle.
4. **Practice independently.**	Encourage students to apply the skill on their own in order to transfer the skill to other activities, including homework assignments.
5. **Share and review.**	Give students a chance to discuss what they learned about using the skill and to share the difficulties they experienced independently. Challenge them to consider additional ways that they could teach and share the skill with a family member and to speculate about the ways that the skill could be used in various professions.

Inquiry skills are helpful in stimulating the strengths, skills, and capacities already present within the individual students (i.e., student assets) and local communities (i.e., family and community assets). In fact, we would be hard pressed to create a meaningful homework assignment that does not integrate these skills. However, integrating these skills should not be the primary goal of any meaningful assignment. The skills should always be linked to the in-school content and used in a way that emphasizes their role in the inquiry process. The rationale for integrating these skills centers on the essential habits of mind that we hope all of our students will develop for professional success and personal fulfillment. Integration of these skills helps students to see the connections between their experiences in school and their lives beyond the classroom.

INTRODUCTION TO HOMEWORK DESIGN PLANNING FORM

Now it is time to put the planning pieces together. Form 5.1: Homework Design Planning Form can assist you in thinking through and organizing meaningful homework assignments. The form may seem tedious, but it is crucial for you to be very clear about your thought processes and goals. Once you get into the habit of good practice, you may find yourself filling out certain sections of the form more than others.

Form 5.1 Homework Design Planning Form

Principles of Meaningful Homework		Inquiry Skills
Check those that are incorporated.		*Check those that will be utilized.*
☐ Providing for expanded meaningfulness and life application of school learning		☐ Ask questions.
☐ Constructing meaning in natural ways and expanding a sense of self-efficacy		☐ Identify problems.
		☐ Collect and analyze data.
☐ Extending education to the home and community by engaging adults in interesting and responsible ways		☐ Make observations.
		☐ Choose sources and collect evidence.
☐ Taking advantage of the students' diversity by using it as a learning resource		☐ Summarize findings and reflect.
☐ Personalizing the curriculum and reflecting on the here and now		☐ _____
☐ Exploiting learning opportunities that are not cost-effective on school time		☐ _____
		☐ _____
☐ Keeping the curriculum up-to-date		

Relevant Standards (national, state, and/or district)

Assignment Goals

Assignment Description

Assignment Timeline

←   →

Assignment Sent Home   **Final Product Due**

Student Assets	Family Assets	Community Assets

Student Input and Voice

Communication With Families	**Necessary Organizational Tools and Resources**
Check those that will be used.	*List those that will be needed.*
☐ Letter to go home	
☐ Open house planned	
☐ E-mail to be sent	
☐ Phone calls	
☐ Home visits	
☐ Classroom Web page to be used	
☐ Inclusion in classroom newsletter	
☐ Student planner	
☐ _____	
☐ _____	
☐ _____	

Instructional Uses of Assignment

Possible Extensions

Integration

☐ Collaboration with another teacher(s) required.

Anticipated Barriers

You may experience resistance from families, administration, or colleagues as you work to change the homework culture in your classroom. A thorough plan will help you to articulate the need for change clearly should such challenges from others arise.

Suggestions on how to use each section of the Homework Design Planning Form follow.

Principles of Meaningful Homework and Inquiry Skills

A beginning point in the planning process may be to decide what principles of meaningful homework and what inquiry skills the assignment will highlight. Depending on the assignment and the goals, it may be possible to focus on just one principle and one inquiry skill, or it may be necessary to include several. Make sure students have a firm understanding of and confidence in any skills they will need to use as they proceed through the homework assignment.

Relevant Standards

Standards afford teachers a starting place from which learning can be extended, expanded, and made meaningful. Teachers may find freedom in knowing the expectations and then "putting the meat on the bones" through rigorous and relevant home assignments that go beyond the basic requirements put forth in the standards. Aspects of the standards are made meaningful to students through the personalization that is found in the types of homework assignments proposed in this text.

Assignment Goals

Homework assignments should match the lesson and unit goals, not just be fun or "something different." They should enrich the curriculum presented in class, giving students a chance to see how what they learn in school actually works in the world around them.

Assignment Description

In this section of the form, explain the general parameters of the assignment. Questions to consider might include the following:

- What will the final product of this assignment look like?
- Will students work in groups, with partners, or independently?
- Who is the intended audience of the final product?

Besides lesson or unit goals, consider level of difficulty, feasibility, and cost-effectiveness. Motivational value, higher-order thinking, and variability should also figure into the decision-making mix. Over time, home assignments should contain a variety of formats and student-response modes. Providing variety over a range of home assignments suited to the unit's goals is a way to accommodate individual differences in students' activity preferences. You might build options into an assignment in terms of communication modes (e.g., reading, writing, speaking, and listening) or information-processing requirements and task forms (e.g., communicating, understanding, responding critically, conducting inquiry, solving problems, and making decisions).

Assignment Timeline

To achieve a mental image of the time frame of the assignment, it may be helpful to sketch a timeline. From when the assignment is sent home to when the final product is due, map out the milestones in between. How long will the assignment take—a day? a week? a month? Will students be required to bring in data halfway through the assignment? Are there checkpoints that should be mapped? Get yourself and your time organized by recording the sequencing of the assignment.

Assets

In the planning-and-design stage of meaningful homework, it is beneficial to consider the assets that already exist in your classroom. These assets can be broken into three categories: student, family, and community.

Student Voice and Choice

Teachers should incorporate student voice and choice when doing so will support the overall goals. For example, some students may choose to write their final product, while others may choose to present it in a video format. Some might go beyond the basic requirements by surveying more people or interviewing additional subjects.

Communication With Families

To maximize the potential that meaningful homework assignments have to improve student performance, give careful thought to communicating with students' families. Begin by promoting change in the culture of how homework is done. It is no longer considered "cheating" for families to work with students on homework assignments; it is necessary and even vital to the learning process. Be clear with families that they are not expected to teach curriculum that was not covered in school; rather they are to collaborate with their children in a joint effort to make learning meaningful. The goals of the assignment must be clearly communicated to ensure a rich experience for all parties.

Necessary Organizational Tools and Resources

List the organizational tools that students will need to complete the homework assignment. Organizational tools may include data collection forms that have been designed by the teacher or co-constructed with students. For example, if the students are surveying individuals, design a form that will make it easy to retrieve and document information. Will the results be tallied, charted, or graphed, for example? If students are simply to carry on a conversation about a specific topic, such as a current event, design a form to document anecdotal information.

In addition to the necessary organizational tools, are there other resources that students will need? For instance, will they need access to a library, computer, or other technology?

Instructional Uses of Assignment

In designing homework, visualize how the activity will be carried out. If a product such as a list or chart will result, how will the information be used as part of subsequent lessons? Will diversity of opinion/perspective be examined simply through in-class discussion, or will a diagram be used? Be flexible, open to modification, and prepared to make pedagogical shifts as needed, but start with a clear plan. The most important thing to remember is to *use* the homework! Even homework that is turned in late can be used as a review or to show how the class data changes with late additions. It provides an opportunity to show how vital each member of the classroom community is; everyone's data is necessary.

Possible Extensions

Assignments often are given to expand, enrich, or reinforce the original task. Though it can be helpful to brainstorm possible extensions, leave room for students to follow their own leads into other areas of interest. It also is possible to generate extensions through classroom discussion. After looking at and discussing the final products of the homework, students may have other areas of inquiry to pursue. Extensions to a well-designed homework assignment will flow naturally if students are given freedom to follow through on their own questions that spring from it.

Integration

Integration is a natural by-product of meaningful homework and often occurs seamlessly. Other opportunities for integration may present themselves with little additional effort on the part of the teacher. Multiple lesson and unit goals from one or more subject areas can be addressed with one home assignment as long as integration does not displace the assignment's primary goals.

Meaningful homework assignments also can provide a common ground on which teachers can work collaboratively. Is there opportunity to work with a teacher from another discipline? Might the fine arts teacher work with the mathematics teacher? The social studies teacher with the science teacher? The collaborative design of meaningful homework assignments offers a chance to build collegiality and tap into the resources and assets that can be found within your school.

Anticipated Barriers

It is always beneficial to anticipate the barriers that could present themselves during the time frame of a meaningful homework assignment. Take a proactive stance to address possible challenges before they occur. Questions to consider might include the following:

- Do my students have access to all the necessary materials (e.g., calculator, computer, Internet, adult collaborators, transportation)?
- How will I help English language learner (ELL) students?
- Do I have struggling readers?
- Do adaptations need to be made for learning-disabled students or gifted students?

REFERENCES

Brophy, J., & Alleman, J. (1991). Activities as instructional tools: A framework for analysis and evaluation. *Educational Researcher, 20,* 9–23.

Moll, L., Amanti, C., Neff, D., & Gonzalez, N. (2001). Funds of knowledge for teaching: Using a qualitative approach to connect homes and classrooms. *Theory Into Practice, 31,* 132–141.

Zais, R. (1976). *Curriculum: Principles and foundations.* New York: Harper and Row.

6

How Can You Put Meaningful Homework Into Action?

In Appendix A, we have provided a completed homework design planning form developed for an assignment focusing on labor unions. The sample form shows how a contemporary issue can be used to support a homework assignment that humanizes content and connects the school's curriculum to students' lives outside the classroom. With this example, we emphasize the importance of integrating events or issues into your homework assignments that are significant to your students and families at the time the assignment is given. Unions and the auto industry were important to this classroom in Michigan during a period when the state was struggling economically. The assignment can be modified to reflect trends or events in other places at other times.

HOMEWORK DESIGN PLANNING

As you begin to create authentic homework assignments, there are numerous decisions to be made. Those decisions affect what happens before students go home, while they are at home, and when the assignment is brought back to school. These decisions are discussed below.

Before Students Go Home

Communication

Communicating with families can be the key to having all of your students complete a meaningful homework assignment successfully. These assignments can look and feel different from the more traditional assignments that parents are familiar with. Therefore, set the tone early in the year and at the beginning of each assignment by communicating to families how valuable these assignments will be for their child and for the entire learning community.

The following letter is an example of how you might begin the homework conversation with families:

Dear Parents:

Each year, every teacher in our school district is required to expand his or her professional repertoire by selecting a goal that goes beyond what is expected to be successful in the classroom. Teachers are encouraged to pick an area that needs attention as evidenced by low student performance. I have chosen meaningful homework.

Recently I read a book entitled *Homework Done Right*, authored by teachers, which has really changed my thinking about homework. I have decided to study the homework I assign and reshape some of my practices. My goal is to make your child's school life more meaningful and compelling. I would be happy to share the book with you.

As I begin to reshape some of my practices, you will notice the following changes:

- Basic skills will not go away. Rather, they will be combined with opportunities for your child to use these skills in real-life situations.
- Most of the homework assignments will *not* have simple right or wrong answers. Instead, they will involve higher-order thinking and real-life application of knowledge and skills.
- If I determine that your child needs guided practice or other traditional homework assignments, they will be provided. Individual students will get whatever additional practice they need.
- You will be encouraged to talk with your child about the assignment, then jump in to provide a helping hand. This will *not* be considered cheating!
- You will be encouraged to participate in homework by adding your views/opinions/observations or sharing your experiences. Your responses will be appreciated and will make our in-school conversations even more enlightening.
- Your child will be expected to complete the assignments in a timely manner, not simply for a score in the grade book but for use during in-class discussions to make the curricular content more meaningful.
- The assignment will not always be graded in the traditional sense. However, its completion will be recorded. I am hoping for a higher level of interest in the subject matter and more active learner participation, with long-term benefits resulting in increased achievement.
- The homework assignments will be aligned with existing curricular goals. They are intended to add meaning to content that students often find dry or unnecessary.
- You can expect frequent homework updates through e-mails, weekly newsletters, and notes that accompany the home assignments. I encourage you to contact me at any time with your questions, concerns, or observations. While it will take time, I'm expecting heightened student interest and ownership in school subjects, leading to higher levels of achievement!

Thank you in advance for engaging with your child and with me in this homework challenge. I believe it has immense promise.

Sincerely,

Ms. Jones

Modeling

As you begin to organize and plan meaningful assignments, visualize the completed assignment and anticipate difficulties that might prevent students from being successful. Then discuss the upcoming tasks with the class and model working through the difficulties. Share the goals for the homework as well as how the data or product will be used.

Modeling the steps of the assignment for students gives them concrete strategies to call upon as they work independently at home. Modeling is most helpful when the actual assignment steps are followed, using the real materials needed.

Keep the modeling as close to reality as possible. For example, if the assignment requires the student to interview someone, ask a colleague to step into the role and demonstrate the interview exchange in class. This is also the time to discuss the problems that students might encounter. Have them participate in problem-solving their way through possible situations, because they will need these skills while completing their own assignment.

The simplest way to model is to begin your own response to the assignment in class. Discuss possible variations and show potential end products. Be thoughtful about this so that students don't merely copy or mimic the example that is modeled for them.

Student Organization

Help students plan for success during the early stages of the assignment. One strategy that will help to promote student planning is table talk, where students discuss the assignment as a group. Verbalizing the steps and how to accomplish them can give students the confidence to get the assignment started right away. A similar strategy is pair-share, where two students put their heads together to brainstorm ideas. This strategy provides an "assignment buddy" to help with motivation and check in with occasionally for the duration of the assignment.

Role-playing is another way to have students work through the steps of the assignment and begin to plan their own work. The teacher can strategically select students who might struggle with the assignment at home to participate in the role-play.

Breaking longer assignments into multiple steps can support students who are at risk for not completing the assignment. Creating multiple deadlines for each part of the assignment provides a natural way to organize the tasks and help students keep track of their own progress.

Teachers can also provide organizers for students to use. Charts, tables, or lists can be sent home as part of the assignment and used to organize data being collected. Two-pocket folders, planners, and file folders are other organizational tools that can support the students as they work through the parts of an assignment.

Motivation and Buy-In

If the teacher communicates how important the assignment is to the individual student, the class as a whole, and to the students' families, they will all be more motivated to invest in it. By participating in the assignment, teachers not only model how to be successful but also show that they value the assignment and are willing to put their own time into completing it. Timely feedback also can persuade students to complete the assignment and return it to school on time.

At Home

Participation

One ultimate goal of any homework assignment is to have 100 percent of the class complete it and bring the final product back to school to share it. Meaningful homework shares this lofty goal, and it has qualities that encourage students to be successful in greater numbers.

If an assignment timeline extends longer than a day or two or has more than one step, teachers can use several techniques to ensure student participation and monitor progress. Chunking the assignment into several parts with different deadlines provides multiple opportunities to check in and problem-solve with students. Teachers can develop a timeline or calendar with students at the beginning of the assignment to clarify the different deadlines and the expectations for each.

During the course of the assignment, students can share the progress of their work. Simple, quick check-in questions can allow teachers to monitor whether students have begun the assignment and are making the expected progress. Even simply asking which family member is assisting with the homework can provide a wealth of information.

For more in-depth information gathering, individual student conferences can be helpful to make certain that students understand the assignment and evaluate the amount of work accomplished. Conferences also allow for teachers to support students through troubleshooting. Even a well-planned and organized assignment may have unexpected problems, and by checking in with students throughout a long-term assignment, teachers can help them to be successful. Waiting until the final deadline to find out that a student encountered a difficult roadblock can be disheartening for both the student and the teacher.

Another technique to encourage 100 percent participation is to have students share parts of their work along the way. Having students bring pieces of their work to show the class or work with an "assignment buddy" can provide ways to monitor progress and provide support for students who need ideas or inspiration.

Family Involvement

Teachers can encourage families to participate in homework by getting the word out that students will need help in various ways throughout the year. Families could chat while driving home from a sporting event or on the way to a scout meeting or while doing household chores together. When designing assignments, teachers can create roles for family members such as information resource, brainstorming partner, or sounding board for new ideas. This practice has the added benefit of often strengthening family relationships. Inviting feedback on assignments is another way to change perceptions about the role of families in the homework process.

Often, these assignments encourage families to interact in positive ways, such as by sharing political opinions or telling stories related to family history. For some families, these are things that used to be done regularly but have become neglected in today's busy society.

Home Visits

Spending time building relationships with your students will often translate into more student engagement and increased participation in meaningful homework assignments. Visiting a student at home can build your relationship with the student, as well as provide you with crucial information about the home situation in relation to homework. You can gather information about which family members could help the student with homework, what resources are available, and whether there is a quiet place to work. This is an ideal opportunity to take stock of a student's family assets as you engage in conversation with the family about the talents, gifts, and strengths of the child.

Back at School

Using the Products of Meaningful Homework

Imagine working hard to complete a homework assignment, gathering information, and returning it to school on time. You carefully place it in the homework basket or bin and then . . . you don't hear anything until weeks later, when it is returned with a grade on the top. No discussion, no feedback, no excitement. It's no wonder that students sometimes feel less than enthusiastic about continuing to participate in homework assignments.

Homework needs to be closely connected to what students have been learning and discussing in class. It should be an extension of what has been learned and should provide an opportunity for students to cement their understandings of the big ideas. Meaningful homework assignments provide an opportunity for students to apply what they've learned and expand their knowledge base.

If your homework is closely aligned with the goals of your daily lessons, homework should become a valuable source of information, brainstorming ideas, data, or other supports. Share with students ahead of time how you plan to use the assignment (e.g., as a tool for contemporizing classroom discussion or as an authentic product).

Inviting an audience into the classroom to view the products of an authentic assignment is one way to use the work done within homework assignments. Authentic homework assignments involve students creating products that the teacher can then use in the classroom in many ways. For example, you might have students create math problems that the class solves or combine student papers into a class book. Other ways to use meaningful homework assignments include classroom displays, newsletters, data for charts, and simply as a means to revisit a lesson narrative and reaffirm the goals of the lesson.

Evaluating the Assignment

> **Example Co-constructed Rubric**
>
> Did I explain my purpose to my interviewee?
>
> Did I ask clear questions?
>
> Did I gather some rich data?
>
> Was I able to share at least one idea with my peers?

Because the focus is on learning rather than compliance, assessing or grading meaningful assignments can look very different from the norm. One possibility is to have the class co-construct a simple rubric that includes all the parts of an assignment. Classroom discussion should include depiction of a high-quality product for students to work toward as they complete the homework.

However, not every assignment needs to be graded. One alternative is to assign a grade for completion. Another is to have students self-assess their assignments with emphasis on elements of the rubric that they co-construct. Another is to create a homework portfolio to demonstrate students' growth and provide a visual representation of that growth to be shared with families during conferences. Assignments need to be valued, so this practice might need to be adopted gradually because it represents a major shift for many people who have long equated value and grades.

Showcasing and Celebrating

For each assignment that you send home, recognize and celebrate the work your students have done. Unfortunately, we usually spend more time fussing at students who haven't turned in the assignment than we do appreciating the students who have worked hard and completed it on time. If you recognize students each time they turn in the homework, you are more likely to motivate them to participate.

There are as many ways to showcase and celebrate student work as there are classrooms. A few examples would be cheering or ringing a chime as they turn it in, placing the work on a bulletin board, or even a simple "Thank you." The important thing is that celebration or recognition happens regularly when students return homework. This may seem corny or time consuming, but students of all ages appreciate being recognized for their effort and the work they've completed.

Displaying the homework is another way to showcase students' efforts, especially when you can tie the display back to the goals of the task. For example, if students have been learning about another country or part of the world, creating a display with a map surrounded by information makes sense, recognizes students' hard work, and helps reinforce the goals of your lessons.

In some assignments, students are generating ideas, not products, so plan to recognize and showcase these ideas. Often, ideas can be more important than products because they clearly demonstrate what students think and understand. Creating a brainstormed list of student ideas is one way to showcase each person's contribution.

If the assignment is extended over a longer period of time with multiple parts, showcase and celebrate the work that students have done so far by sharing and recording the ideas they've completed. Students who haven't finished the work can see the ideas and get excited about participating in the assignment themselves.

Finally, be sure that the showcasing and celebrating doesn't overshadow the importance of the assignment itself. In the end, it is important to have students participate, learn, and grow from each meaningful assignment.

> **Example**
> **Co-constructed Rubric**
>
> Did I ask specific questions?
>
> Did I use follow-up probes in order to acquire rich data?
>
> Did I look for patterns as I was analyzing data?
>
> Did I draw some tentative conclusions?

> **Example**
> **Co-constructed Rubric**
>
> Did I use more than one source?
>
> Did I attempt to use a range of different types of sources?
>
> Did I attempt to find sources that varied in perspectives?

ACCOUNTABILITY: SETTING STANDARDS AND EXPECTATIONS

It is important to establish early in the year that all students are expected to participate in *all* homework assignments. If you tell students how their grade will be affected by not completing homework, they will see those assignments as optional and begin to make decisions about whether or not to participate. On the other hand, if you make it clear that all assignments must and will be completed by all students, they will begin to understand that not turning in the homework isn't an option.

Communicate early as you introduce the assignment and frequently throughout it. Discuss *why* this assignment is important. If we can convince students that homework has value to them, they will be more engaged in the assignment and more successful in completing it. Help your students answer the following two questions to motivate them to participate and be successful with any homework assignment: What's in it for me? Will I be successful with this assignment?

A great way to communicate the value of the assignment is for you to complete it along with the class. When students see their teacher working, interviewing, researching, or writing to finish the same work they are doing, they know it is important. Students will appreciate the effort and often look forward to seeing your answers. They will be more engaged and excited about the assignment knowing that you are willing to join in the fun!

Deadlines can be a key component to any homework assignment. Once again, establishing clear expectations and then communicating those expectations to students and their families is important. Learning to meet deadlines is an important life skill that goes way beyond any homework assignment.

To help with this, create a reasonable timeline for the assignment. Asking students to help create the timeline can motivate them to meet the deadlines. It is also important to stick to the deadlines that you've established. Shifting deadlines or other expectations can be confusing for students and cause misunderstanding and frustration. When unforeseen circumstances present themselves and potentially impact the assignment deadline, having a discussion about requests for modifying the project timeline is a reasonable approach.

Turning in homework assignments late is a difficult, often controversial topic. However, from the perspective of meaningful homework, it is better for the student to complete the homework late than never do it at all, despite the fact that it then becomes difficult to include in class discussion. Therefore, take time to work with students to find out why an assignment is late and how you can support that student to complete the assignment.

ASSESSING THE HOMEWORK ASSIGNMENT

After all is said and done, take time to assess the overall worth and value of the homework assignment itself. Looking at the various parts of the assignment and its purpose, make informed decisions about keeping, dropping, or modifying the assignment with another class or in another year.

Using a homework planning tool like the form in Chapter 5 during the planning stages can be an effective way to reflect on the value and benefits of the task. Look at the results of the homework and compare them to the original intent of the assignment. The question to begin with is, was this assignment successful? However, there can be much more to consider.

For example, did noteworthy patterns emerge? How many students participated? What was their level of excitement and engagement? Which skills did they use? These are areas where you can gather data and suggestions directly from your students. This is another valuable way for students to have their voices heard.

Be sure to go back to the design factors. Check to see if your assignment met the goals selected at the beginning. This analysis will help support the changes made in your homework program as well as help you refine the next assignment you plan to design.

In conclusion, the topics discussed throughout this chapter support meaningful homework in different ways. Some of the pieces are easier to adapt and use than others. Changing homework philosophy and beginning to adjust assignments shouldn't be an overwhelming prospect. As you begin to take the first steps, read through the possible assignments in the next section. Whether the assignment is suggested for your grade level or not, you will find activities that can be modified and used to make your homework more meaningful.

Part III

Examine the Possibilities

The intent of Part III is to connect you with children and adolescents by describing the general nature of the learner and the importance of homework at each grade level. You will notice that as the learner develops and changes, the approaches to and emphases of homework may also shift. In each of the chapters, designated by grade levels (i.e., early elementary, upper elementary, middle school, and high school), the authors have provided examples from each of the four core areas along with selected examples from electives.

Each example is aligned with one or more principles of meaningful homework, with specific curricular goals, and with national curriculum standards drawn from the respective subject area organizations. Our selections aren't intended to be limiting, so you may see others we did not include. The extended example in each section includes context to help you visualize what is going on in the classroom, prerequisite skills to illustrate the essential processes students need at their fingertips to be successful with the assignment, and cross talk.

The short examples include all of the same components plus daily and long-term assignments with extensions. Reviewing and reflecting on multiple examples in each chapter should give you a vivid picture of the possibilities so you can begin crafting assignments that match your content goals. You might use the examples as they are, modify or select pieces that apply to your content area, or use our examples simply as thought starters.

You will find it helpful to read all four chapters of Part III. The early grades tend to be long on strategy and activities and short on content, but this reverses by the time students reach fourth grade. Content often becomes overwhelming, and time spent on strategy/activity is minimized. As an adult, you probably have experienced the joy of playful moments doing something elementary, as well as feeling good about doing something you originally thought was beyond your scope. With that in mind, we ask you to shift your paradigms and begin thinking about broad possibilities, while always adhering to your content goals.

We provide cross talk at the end of each example as another way of engaging you and helping you anticipate the challenges you might face as you tackle possibly "outside-the-box" assignments. Each author has weighed in on the responses to share multiple perspectives and to trigger possible applications for you across grade levels.

7

How Can Meaningful Homework Look in the Early Elementary Grades?

Barbara Knighton

WHY IS HOMEWORK IMPORTANT TO THE EARLY ELEMENTARY LEARNER?

Early elementary students need teachers to help them build a solid foundation of content information in the early stages of a unit. They often have very little prior knowledge or knowledge that is full of misconceptions, so introductions to new units or topics should have more direct instruction. Reviewing the new information during home assignments can help students retain it in their long-term memories.

Young children also need extra support in making connections between new information and things they've learned in other lessons and other content areas. Teachers need to be specific, help students recall information, and then show how it connects to newly acquired concepts. Meaningful homework can be structured to showcase and encourage those connections.

Early elementary students must see and understand how the concepts and skills they are learning are connected to their world. Many will need specific, concrete examples of these connections. Homework assignments should be designed to have children practice skills learned at school in real-life situations in their homes.

Recording information during instruction to co-construct learning materials helps children recall and use the information on the co-constructed charts and posters in the future. Creating the posters, charts, lists, or tables together as a class helps the students understand where the information comes from and how it connects together. Re-creating those posters, charts, or tables at home as part of an authentic assignment is a wonderful way for them to solidify their understanding of the information, share it with their families, and show their grasp of the concepts.

Finally, younger students need practice with hands-on materials to see and manipulate objects related to the concepts they are learning. In many cases, it isn't feasible or time- and cost-efficient to bring those materials into the classroom for extended hands-on learning opportunities, but home assignments can provide additional occasions for students to use them.

EXTENDED EXAMPLE: EARLY ELEMENTARY SOCIAL STUDIES—MY ANCESTORS

Principles of Meaningful Homework

- Providing for expanded meaningfulness and life application of school learning
- Extending education to the home and community by engaging adults in interesting and responsible ways

National Standard

Individual Development and Identity

Assignment Goal(s)

- ✓ Students will understand and appreciate their own ancestry and country of origin.
- ✓ Students will apply knowledge of family history by recording anecdotes.
- ✓ Students will apply writing and reading skills to meaningful, personalized content.

In-School Context

Most early elementary social studies programs include a unit on families. In this classroom, the students participated in a particularly robust family unit that included learning about the history of families, cultural and geographic influences on families, and economic studies related to family purchases. There have been several lessons on the historical development of the family unit and roles within families. The lessons begin with the life and family of the teacher, then shift to examples from the lives of the students in the class, and finally consider children and families from around the world. Conversations center first on ways that families are the same and then move to understanding and appreciating the differences.

The current lesson is about extended families and ancestors. Part of the discussion will include information and examples about immigrants, focusing on the reasons they move to new countries.

Inquiry Skills

- Ask questions.
- Collect and analyze data.
- Summarize findings and reflect.

Description of Assignment

The first assignment asked students to find out what countries represented their ancestry. They discussed where each country is located on the globe and what family traditions relate to it. After students brought the information to school, the class placed sticker dots on a map to show the information. This initial assignment opened the door to discoveries about the students' ancestors and piqued interest in the history of their own families. Then, over the course of a week, students took home a series of questions to ask family members as they assembled a portfolio of family stories and information. Questions included inquiries about immigrant ancestors, countries of ancestry, reasons for immigration, family traditions, and cultures brought to America. Questions such as "How did I get my name?" or "How do my ancestors affect my life today?" focused on the student's place in the family. As a final project, students created a book of family information.

At the end of the unit, they invited their families to attend a special Open House at the school. In preparation, they created invitations and planned which artifacts from the lessons to display for families to investigate. Families signed up to bring refreshments related to their ethnic cultures and traditions. The final event of the evening was a celebration of the stories the children had collected along with opportunities to read the stories. For the data collection tool that the students used in this assignment, see Appendix B.1.

Cross Talk Questions

1. What will I do for children who don't know their ancestry and have no one to interview?

   B.B.   *Contact a local organization, the school's parent/teacher organization, or adults throughout your school for assistance.*

   J.A.   *Have students investigate the country that represents their ancestry. Students might talk with family members about a custom from people of that country that they would like to adopt.*

2. How do I support struggling writers and young readers through this assignment?

   J.A.   *Encourage students to tape the interviews. Recruit volunteers to do transcriptions.*

   R.L.   *Allow students to express their ancestry through other modes of expression such as illustrations of flags, the country's symbols, or other representations of family traditions.*

   S.M.   *Use a lot of pictures and examples for students who are nonreaders.*

3. How can I structure the opportunity to share the stories without using too much class time?

   S.M.   *Find a buddy classroom with older students to read with the class.*

   B.K.   *Allow just a few students to share each day until everyone has had a turn. Have each student choose one page to share and then put all the stories into the class library.*

   J.A.   *Use community-building time for sharing the stories. Replace show-and-tell time with the stories, or use some of your literacy time as it seems like a natural fit.*

EARLY ELEMENTARY SCIENCE
WEATHER REPORTING YOU CAN BELIEVE

Principles of Meaningful Homework

- Extending education to the home and community by engaging adults in interesting and responsible ways
- Personalizing the curriculum and reflecting on the here and now

National Standard

Earth and Space Science

Assignment Goal(s)

✓ Students will know several sources of weather information.
✓ Students will understand and apply science and weather vocabulary within assignments.

In-School Context

Students in an early elementary science class were just beginning a unit on weather that focused on observing and recording weather by using journals and weather instruments. This assignment is used very early in the unit, possibly even before formal instruction begins. The teacher started by brainstorming the various sources for gathering weather information.

Inquiry Skills

- Ask questions.
- Make observations.
- Choose sources and collect evidence.
- Summarize findings and reflect.

Description of Assignment

- *Short-term:* Students found at least one source of weather information and listed the weather words they heard or read. Each student brought his or her list— which included a description of the source used—to be added to a poster in class. The poster was used as a resource for journal writing later in the unit. As words were added to the list, the class sorted them into categories (e.g., temperature, wind, and precipitation). These categories helped students to organize the structure of their future weather journal entries. Further investigation of this list lead to conversations about connections between categories. For the data collection tool that the students used in this assignment, see Appendix B.2.

- *Long-term:* Over the several weeks of the weather unit, students were asked to explore several sources of weather information with their families. Each week they looked at a different source, including televised weather reports, newspaper forecasts, and the National Weather Service Forecast online (www.crh.noaa.gov). As they gathered weather words, they were asked to analyze sources through questions such as these: Which source gives you the most useful information? Which source is easiest to understand? Which source can you find whenever you need it? Finally, after observing and recording weather in their school journals for several weeks, students chose one of these sources to replicate, using their data. They presented a TV weather report in class, designed a newspaper page, or used a computer to create a Web site weather forecast.

Extensions

- Make connections with local meteorologists; have students write questions to ask.
- Draw weather pictures with captions.
- Survey people to find out which weather source they use most often, then analyze responses by location, age of respondent, or purpose of source use.

Cross Talk Questions

1. If I choose to give this assignment before the unit starts, would students have enough accurate prior knowledge to make it successful?

   S.M. *Use this assignment to assess prior knowledge of the students. Use it to know where to start and move them forward from there.*

   J.A. *Explain expectations ahead of time so family members support this assignment as a way to build knowledge. This would prevent misunderstandings and bad PR.*

2. How do I support struggling writers and young readers through this assignment?

   B.B. *Search for auditory and/or visual sources such as a television broadcast or a newspaper page with pictures. Then steer those students in that direction as they choose their sources.*

   J.A. *Encourage them to have conversations with family members that focus on environmental print. This will also promote future interest in reading.*

3 In the long-term example, should every student be required to perform/present his or her final project?

   S.M. *Because classroom celebrations are really important, everyone must participate.*

   R.L. *Everyone should be required to participate. Assign it early enough that it would create a purpose for learning.*

   J.A. *Allow students to incorporate their ideas and choose how they will deliver the final product, without changing the expectations.*

4. How should I structure sharing the final project?

   B.B. *Look for ways to involve the students in the presentation so they are an active audience.*

   R.L. *Schedule a family night to provide an audience and include families in the project and the presentations.*

   J.A. *Break the class into several small groups and send the groups to perform in other classrooms.*

EARLY ELEMENTARY SOCIAL STUDIES—THE CLOTHING MUSEUM

Principles of Meaningful Homework

- Constructing meaning in natural ways and expanding a sense of self-efficacy
- Extending education to the home and community by engaging adults in interesting and responsible ways
- Exploiting learning opportunities that are not cost-effective on school time

National Standard

Production, Distribution, and Consumption

Assignment Goal(s)

✓ Students will understand the origins, uses, and fabrics of the clothing in their closets.
✓ Students will apply concepts to clothing in their lives.

In-School Context

Students in an early elementary social studies class are nearing the end of a unit on the cultural universal of clothing. They've learned about the reasons for wearing clothes and different types of specialized clothing, they've discussed purchasing clothing and the choices people can make, and they know about different kinds of fabric and how they are manufactured. Class discussions have included geographic influences on clothing as well as the global influences on supply, demand, and availability. In this assignment, they will orchestrate the information acquired during the unit as they search their closets at home.

Inquiry Skills

- Collect and analyze data.
- Make observations.
- Summarize findings and reflect.

Description of Assignment

- *Short-term:* Each student brought one piece of clothing from his or her home and prepared a short (i.e., 3- to 5-minute) oral presentation to share information about the clothing item. The presentations included information from the tags such as where the item was purchased, proper care of the item, and the cost of the item. Students showed the item to the class and gave information about it related to the big ideas they learned throughout the unit. Each piece of clothing then became part of the classroom Clothing Museum to demonstrate what was learned throughout the unit. Family members came to tour the museum and see the different articles of clothing.

- *Long-term:* Over the final week, students helped to generate a list of items to search for in their closets at home—items directly connected to lessons taught during the unit. As the teacher reviewed each part of the unit, the class brainstormed items to add to the "clothing hunt" list. At the end of the weeklong review, the list was typed and sent home with students. They used the list and their knowledge of clothing to locate each item. The list included a rubric to help them assess their progress. Examples on the list included garments worn on special occasions, uniforms, items worn for protection, items manufactured in other parts of the world, items sewn by hand and therefore considered one of a kind, items mass-produced, items made from natural fibers, items made from synthetic fibers, etc. There were so many possible ways of categorizing articles of clothing! For the data collection tool that the students used in this assignment, see Appendix B.3.

Extensions

- Use tag information from clothing to connect with math instruction on fractions or percentages.
- Organize a clothing drive or other charitable plan, such as knitting baby caps.
- Connect with a local drama club to explore and analyze play costumes.
- Use the data gathered to create pictographs or other data analyses.
- Take students on a virtual tour of another museum to compare with the class museum.

Cross Talk Questions

1. How will I organize the Clothing Museum?

    S.M.   *Have students wear their favorite items and become living models.*

    B.B.   *Get access to a used mannequin and put items on as they come to school.*

2. How can I ensure a variety of examples in the museum?

    B.B.   *Begin with a bowl of paper slips with words such as head, feet, etc. Choose one slip each week or day and have students focus on clothing for that body part.*

    S.M.   *Create a chart with several categories that have a limited number of spaces. When the spaces are full, students must bring something from another category.*

    J.A.   *Early on, as a class, brainstorm all types of examples. Sort according to function, fabric type, season for wearing, manufacturing location, etc. Ask families to brainstorm other categories of clothing to be represented.*

3. In the long-term example, how can I guarantee/know that students are completing the assignment?

    J.A.   *Connect some kind of data gathering as part of the assignment; the data can be combined to do more analysis in class. This will also lend a level of seriousness to the assignment.*

    B.K.   *Regularly check in with students about their progress. Ask them to give examples of clothing found in their closets.*

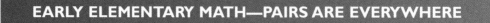

EARLY ELEMENTARY MATH—PAIRS ARE EVERYWHERE

Principles of Meaningful Homework

- Providing for expanded meaningfulness and life application of school learning
- Personalizing the curriculum and reflecting on the here and now

National Standard

Number and Operations

Assignment Goal(s)

- ✓ Students will appreciate and apply ways to use the skill of counting by twos in their daily lives.
- ✓ Students will understand pictorial representations of a math concept.

In-School Context

Students in an early elementary class had been learning the concept that some things are naturally found in pairs and other things are grouped in twos. They had been practicing counting by twos and had discussed the patterns found in numbers when counting. The teacher modeled the skill and guided the class through several opportunities to practice counting groups of objects by twos. Then the class focused on the relevance of this skill by examining the world around them for things that come in groups of two, therefore creating the necessity of counting by twos.

Inquiry Skills

- Ask questions.
- Collect and analyze data.
- Make observations.

Description of Assignment

- *Short-term:* Students searched their homes and other places for things that come in groups of two. With their family, they created a list of those things and practiced counting them by twos. From the list, they chose one example to sketch and label with numbers to show the skill of counting by twos. Then they added a sentence below the picture to tell about the pairs (e.g., "Bicycle wheels come in pairs."). The sentence provided the text for a page in the class book that was created at school. For the data collection tool that the students used in this assignment, see Appendix B.4.

- *Long-term:* The class was encouraged to explore the community in which they lived and to identify items that require counting by twos. When several items were identified, the class made a poster that represented their findings. As students talked with family members using the completed poster as a conversation starter, the teacher led class discussions about the usefulness of the skill of counting by twos. She then encouraged students to talk with adults they knew in the community about the importance of learning to count by twos.

Extensions

- Find things that can be broken into groups of two.
- Find objects in groups of 3s, 5s, and 10s.
- Explore the idea of things that seem to come in pairs but aren't really pairs (e.g., opposites).

Cross Talk Questions

1. Which should I teach first, the concept that things come in pairs or the skill of counting by twos?

    R.L.   *Find things at school that come in pairs to teach the rote counting skills. In other words, teach both together.*

    B.B.   *Use naturally occurring pairs as a springboard for the skill of counting by twos.*

2. How does the teacher communicate the long-term assignment to families and maintain student focus and interest in the assignment over time?

    J.A.   *Write a letter to families explaining the goals, intended results, etc. Make sure you include concrete examples to stimulate family discussions and to provide direction for the home assignments. Periodically have students bring in objects and explain conversations with help from family members.*

    S.M.   *Model the long-term assignment over the course of a day where you can show examples from around the room.*

    R.L.   *Communicate up front with the families about the end product.*

3. What examples should be modeled at school? How do you encourage students to look for examples beyond the first few obvious ones like eyes, ears, and body parts?

    J.A.   *Take some photos of examples outside of school and model writing a paragraph or description. Brainstorm a list of possibilities and add to it as you go along.*

    R.L.   *Provide areas or themes around which students can focus their ideas. Look for student input into the themes. Then sort and organize the ideas into a Bingo-like chart. Students need to find examples for each category, such as body parts, toys, clothing, etc.*

EARLY ELEMENTARY ENGLISH LANGUAGE ARTS—TRAVELING MASCOT

Principles of Meaningful Homework

- Providing for expanded meaningfulness and life application of school learning
- Constructing meaning in natural ways and expanding a sense of self-efficacy
- Extending education to the home and community by engaging adults in interesting and responsible ways

(Continued)

(Continued)

National Standard

Students adjust their use of spoken, written, and visual language (e.g., conventions, style, vocabulary) to communicate effectively with a variety of audiences and for different purposes. Students employ a wide range of strategies as they write and use different writing process elements appropriately to communicate with different audiences for a variety of purposes.

Assignment Goal(s)

✓ Students will apply writing and recording skills to create journal entries.
✓ Students will understand personal narrative structures.

In-School Context

One challenge for an early elementary teacher is getting students to spend more time writing and recording the events of their lives. Teachers especially focus on writing personal narratives chronologically from the beginning of the event through the middle to the end. In this classroom, students had the opportunity at school to write every day during Writer's Workshop. However, children rarely got the chance to write stories or journals at home.

When parents work at home with their child, they often feel more comfortable reading to their child or practicing printing skills. These students spent the first two months learning to plan and record personal narratives. They also learned how to identify story ideas and plan them by oral storytelling. They recorded those stories in three parts across the pages of a book. Then they were ready to become more independent and try the process at home.

Inquiry Skills

- Ask questions.
- Make observations.
- Summarize findings and reflect.

Description of Assignment

- *Short-term:* All students recorded an interesting event that occurred at home over the Thanksgiving vacation (e.g., preparing a meal for Thanksgiving, going shopping, visiting a relative, or getting a new pet). With partners, they shared plans for the weekend and then chose one photocopy of a book character from a recent class story. They talked with their partners about how to have the character join their plans. The teacher modeled the thinking process for choosing a story idea and shared a plan out loud for the students to follow. The character was used to help the students focus on the actions during the event. After taking the character home, they had the character mimic their actions as they went through the weekend. Students also took a writing booklet home. Over the weekend, they chose an event to journal about. A family member listened as they planned by storytelling the event's beginning, middle, and end. The student recorded the story, first by drawing pictures and then with words. When students returned to school on Monday, they shared one page from their character's story. Then the stories were collected for each character and put together in a book for the class library.

- *Long-term:* The teacher and students chose a stuffed animal to become the class mascot. The class mascot was the main character in each story in the journal. Early in the year, the mascot was included in class activities. The class discussed the activities and used them to learn about sequencing. The teacher modeled writing journal accounts of the mascot participating in class activities. They included photographs, drawings, souvenirs, and other artifacts to help enhance the story. After the students were successfully recording stories with minimal support, they began taking the mascot home to participate in family activities. They signed up to take turns "hosting" the mascot for a few days at a time. Families chose either a special event for the visit or a few normal days to invite the mascot home. The mascot traveled with a backpack or bag that held the mascot, a spiral journal, writing materials, and all the artifacts from each adventure. While the mascot was at each home, the student created a journal entry in the notebook for each day, focusing on an interesting event from that day. For the data collection tool that the students used in this assignment, see Appendix B.5.

Extensions

- Write and send a postcard from the mascot while it is away from the classroom.
- Use the character for a nonfiction writing activity to provide an opportunity to write for different purposes.
- Encourage families to create their own mascot with a diary.

Cross Talk Questions

1. What management should I consider as I plan to model this activity?

   J.A.   *Role-play lots of possibilities, such as explaining the task to families and sharing the rationale for it.*

   S.M.   *Create a social story to help children know how to care for and use the mascot.*

2. If families choose not to sign up for the mascot, should I send it home anyway?

   R.L.   *If families don't have an assigned time, assign them a turn yourself, communicate ahead of time what to do, and ask for their help.*

   J.A.   *Explain to families in layperson's terms what you are asking them to do and why and how it will be important in the future. Provide lots of concrete examples to illustrate.*

3. How can I encourage family members to support the young writer without taking over the task?

   B.B.   *Direct parents to see the work that other students have done as an example.*

   B.K.   *Be very specific in the directions so that parents understand the expectations.*

8

How Can Meaningful Homework Look in the Upper Elementary Grades?

Rob Ley

WHY IS HOMEWORK IMPORTANT TO THE UPPER ELEMENTARY LEARNER?

Upper elementary students are involved in an important stage of their schooling that positions them like visitors to a new country, attempting to figure out their place within a suddenly complicated culture and system. As an increased quantity of content is presented at a faster rate, they are challenged to disentangle the purposes of school in their lives. The level to which the curriculum is personally framed for students determines how familiar or foreign school becomes for them.

The upper elementary level is the point at which many students' fragile self-concepts are formed and when many of them begin to question the quality of their experience in school. Homework provides an opportunity for upper elementary students to reinforce their role in the curriculum, while applying skills and knowledge in a real-world setting. Due to their growing need to connect personally with new content, an increased sense of peer importance, and a new willingness to share their interests, upper elementary students naturally value assignments and tools that help them organize the world outside of school.

Upper elementary students not only must learn to deal with content overload, but they are also confronted with standardized tests for the first time. These tests take on a life of their own by emphasizing that the purpose of school is to prepare for future grades and to attain grade-level norms. The increased use of standardized assessments, along with the fact that students are often receiving letter grades for the first time, often leads upper elementary learners to view teachers and school in general with suspicion.

Wariness about school increases as students become personally removed from the center of the curriculum. Unlike the early elementary curriculum, which focuses on students and their families, neighborhoods, and communities, upper elementary standards often lack direct connections to the student. A focus on concepts that expands students' consciousness of social issues impacting the family, the community, and the world may generate in these often enthusiastic young people feelings of uneasiness and worry. They frequently carry a deep seriousness for these concerns along with an unrelenting interest in creating fairness. These dispositions can be used to help direct productive inquiry and action outside of school as students and teachers collaboratively try to answer these questions: What is worth knowing? What can we do with that knowledge?

Upper elementary students are able to form genuine learning partnerships with adults as they develop the desire to feel included in adult intellectual activity. Homework is powerful when it speaks to students and parents in ways that reflect their lives and the content being learned. The family's role in school can be re-established during the upper elementary years. During this time, parents ask how they can be most effectively involved with increasingly advanced content and how they can help their child to reason and solve problems with greater independence. When a homework activity becomes worth doing for its own sake, students feel their actions are significant, and they want to involve their parents or other adults in meaningful ways.

Regrettably, when we ignore our upper elementary students' sincere need to find purpose in what we ask of them, they will likely replace their natural curiosity with a mere desire to complete assignments in ways that result in better grades or other rewards. Homework and school in general become counterfeit experiences that are detrimental to both learning goals and appreciation of the purpose of school. The upper elementary level is a critical time to emphasize meaningful homework as a way for students to form active relationships with both the curriculum and the world outside of school.

EXTENDED EXAMPLE: UPPER ELEMENTARY SOCIAL STUDIES EXTENDING DEMOCRACY VIA VOTER REGISTRATION

Principles of Meaningful Homework

- Extending education to the home and community by engaging adults in interesting and responsible ways
- Personalizing the curriculum and reflecting on the here and now
- Keeping the curriculum up-to-date

National Standard

Power, Authority, and Governance

(Continued)

(Continued)

Assignment Goal(s)

✓ Students will understand the importance of voting within a democracy.
✓ Students will understand some of the issues connected to the local, state, and national election.
✓ Students will understand voting trends and attitudes by conducting interviews and a survey of voters in the community.

In-School Context

Throughout a fourth-grade civics and government unit, students had become active participants in and contributors to determining the direction of their classroom study. There was a strong connection between a citizen's role within government and the students' role within the classroom. At various stages throughout the unit, students were empowered to assert their positions on issues, and they had realized the importance of taking a stance within their own learning. The class used basic principles of American democracy to study the purpose and organizational structure of government and the responsibilities of citizenship.

Inquiry Skills

* Ask questions.
* Collect and analyze data.
* Summarize findings and reflect.

Description of Assignment

During a recent election, students contributed to the voting process by seeking out unregistered voters in their community and convincing them of the importance of being involved in the decision-making process of our democracy. This assignment was designed to personalize the content being learned in class as students attempted to answer key questions related to voter registration and turnout in their town.

This assignment could not have been completed in the classroom because students needed to collect information from a large number of people in their community. The assignment was ongoing and lasted two weeks. Students' findings were reported daily and integrated into the unit. Results from the assignment allowed valuable connections to be made between state standards, students' interests, and community issues. For example, a student found out that her parents were registered to vote in a state that they had recently moved from but were not registered in their new state. This created a purpose for studying local and state issues and expanded students' understanding that ballot choices go further than just selecting a presidential candidate.

With a family member, students first examined the PBS-sponsored Web site The Democracy Project: Inside the Voting Booth (http://pbskids.org/democracy/vote). This created a shared content experience with parents. The site is very kid-friendly, with historical photographs that encourage families to generate voting-related questions together. Students and families then made a list of people with whom they could discuss politics. In addition to family members, this list included people in the community such as barbers, bus drivers, and grocery store cashiers. Students then set out to see if those people were registered to vote. They were encouraged to choose people with whom they interacted routinely so that additional arrangements would not be required. Their mission was to talk about issues and ideas by using campaign conversation starters that were modeled and practiced in class. They were prepared to take one of two actions, depending on whether or not the person was registered to vote.

It was as valuable for students to see how many people were already registered to vote as it was for them to register new voters. They were prepared to discuss the importance of taking action in government and to make the argument that voting is essential in a democracy. Students recorded notes about their conversations on a record-keeping hand-out. They also recorded questions that they had after talking with each person and identi-fied government/civic topics they were interested in learning more about. For the data collection tool that the students used in this assignment, see Appendix C.1.

Throughout the voting-registration assignment, students were able to bring a variety of important questions and new insights about elections to their classroom study. New ques-tions about the voting process, history, and current issues were posted daily, and the variety of different people involved in their assignment expanded the diversity of their questions. These questions did not need to be answered immediately, sequentially, or com-prehensively, but they were recorded and referred to throughout the unit. This assignment generated a purpose and a need to learn more.

For example, initially students were puzzled about how to respond to citizens who displayed a lack of interest in voting or people who had negative perceptions of govern-ment. They realized the importance of learning about the historical struggles of many groups of Americans to obtain the right to vote and cleverly used this information in their discussions with others outside of school. Finding out how many voters their class could register also created enthusiasm among students because they did not know how the assignment would turn out. Students felt that they were doing something important and original. They demonstrated a stubborn willingness to continue to find more and more people to talk with, and having a registration deadline brought the assignment to a natural close. Instead of being concerned about a grade or a consequence for not com-pleting the assignment, they became more interested in finding out how many voters they could register. As students learned more about voting, they started to read the newspaper and classroom magazines with greater inquisitiveness and purpose. Classroom discussions also improved as students became not only better informed but more enthusiastic about current issues. They demonstrated an increased capacity to understand complicated issues that the teacher would never have thought of integrating into the unit.

The teacher posted the results of the students' political conversations as well as any additional questions the students had and related topics of interest. Students then used this information to guide their choice of an independent project that examined their chosen topic or issue in greater depth. The finished projects were presented as digital stories.

Cross Talk Questions

1. How can I honor students' and families' different political beliefs while keeping the class-room politically independent?

   B.B. *Explain that people's ideas and beliefs about the world typically change over time. Furthermore, the ability to understand these issues from multiple perspectives is an impor-tant ability to possess.*

(Continued)

(Continued)

> R.L. *Stress from the beginning that the unit is going to focus on important issues related to the election.*

2. How do I support students who encounter apathetic or cynical unregistered voters?

> B.B. *These opportunities allow students to explore the perceived lack of political efficacy that exists within a portion of our society. How does this lack of political efficacy arise? Do these feelings exist for all levels of government? Does this group of individuals have something in common, demographically or otherwise? Why?*

> B.K. *Have mock interviews with another teacher to play the role of the cynical voter.*

3. How can I extend this assignment for students who only find people who are already registered to vote?

> S.M. *Instruct the students to ask interviewees how regularly they vote.*

> B.K. *Instruct the students to ask interviewees about their voting history. How do they find out about candidates and their ideas related to the issues?*

> B.B. *Instruct students to explore reasons why people sometimes are unable to vote. Perhaps neighbors are unable to register to vote because they are immigrants to the United States who have not become naturalized citizens.*

UPPER ELEMENTARY SCIENCE—PUTTING WHEELCHAIR ACCESSIBILITY RIGHTS INTO MOTION

Principles of Meaningful Homework

- Providing for expanded meaningfulness and life application of school learning
- Personalizing the curriculum and reflecting on the here and now

National Standard

Physical Science

Assignment Goal(s)

✓ Students will describe and compare motions of common objects in terms of speed and direction.
✓ Students will understand how forces (e.g., pushes or pulls) are needed to speed up, slow down, stop, or change the direction of a moving object, and they will be able to explain that the greater the force is, the greater the change in motion will be.
✓ Students will appreciate simple machines and describe how they change effort.

In-School Context

Students in third grade had been learning about concepts related to force and motion through a problem-based learning unit. They were becoming aware of various simple machines and had been applying their functions to real-world objects such as a wheelchair. Students were then presented with the following issue:

We are expecting a new student named Abby who uses a wheelchair. The school board is interested in knowing more about the motion of a wheelchair in order to determine whether structural changes need to be made so that all areas of the building are accessible to her. The board is looking into building designs but needs assistance in gathering information about appropriate wheelchair speeds. Abby uses a nonmotorized, four-wheeled wheelchair that she moves by hand. For safety purposes, it is best that she can move at a constant speed, and it is challenging for her to change direction suddenly. What information would be important for us to know about how wheelchairs move?

Students researched how wheelchairs are operated, the laws mandating equality, and the costs for building changes. They planned routes for the student with a physical disability while making sure that their design followed the movement of the rest of the students throughout the school. They also designed a ramp for the school's theatrical stage by analyzing the appropriate speed and direction of wheelchair movement.

Inquiry Skills

- Identify problems.
- Make observations.
- Summarize findings and reflect.

Description of Assignment

- *Short-term:* Students explored how simple machines are used in their daily lives by sketching images of these machines being used to make everyday work in their community easier. They summarized their sketches by writing a reflection on what their life would be like if they did not have simple machines, describing the challenges they would therefore face on a daily basis. For the data collection tool that the students used in this assignment, see Appendix C.2.

- *Long-term:* Students toured local stores and restaurants to see if they were accessible to people with physical disabilities. If necessary, they contacted appropriate officials and shared plans to make these accessible.

Extensions

- Explore a variety of disability issues, including accessibility for the blind or visually impaired.
- Invite speakers from an advocacy group.
- Study the Americans with Disabilities Act and discuss its implications for new construction projects and its impact on existing construction.

Cross Talk Questions

1. How will I prepare students to use their observations to create quality sketches?

    J.A.   *Model, model, model. Co-construct quality sketches. Demonstrate a quality sketch.*

(Continued)

(Continued)

B.B. *Focus attention on the key components of the machine without which it could not serve its purpose, such as the load-bearing portions or the transfer mechanisms.*

B.K. *Together, create a rubric to establish quality observations. Consider using a pictorial example at each level of the rubric. These sketches would communicate the qualities of an effective sketch. You wouldn't need to draw a simple machine but could use another example.*

2. How will I respond if the attempt to create wheelchair-accessible areas in the community is met with resistance from businesses?

B.B. *Explore the costs of such changes. Also, introduce students to the idea of "grandfathering" in regards to these types of changes.*

B.K. *Use this as an opportunity to model and teach children how people can respectfully disagree with each other.*

UPPER ELEMENTARY ENGLISH LANGUAGE ARTS
LOCATING PROBLEMS FOR EDITORIALS

Principles of Meaningful Homework

- Constructing meaning in natural ways and expanding a sense of self-efficacy
- Personalizing the curriculum and reflecting on the here and now

National Standard

Students read a wide range of print and nonprint texts to build an understanding of texts, of themselves, and of the cultures of the United States and the world; to acquire new information; to respond to the needs and demands of society and the workplace; and for personal fulfillment. Among these texts are fiction and nonfiction, classic and contemporary works. Students conduct research on issues and interests by generating ideas and questions and by posing problems. They gather, evaluate, and synthesize data from a variety of sources (e.g., print and nonprint texts, artifacts, people) to communicate their discoveries in ways that suit their purpose and audience.

Assignment Goal(s)

✓ Students will appreciate the importance of problem finding as a prerequisite for op-ed pieces that attempt to influence an intended audience.

✓ Students will find ways to connect personal stories to real-world problems and identify problems in their school and community.

In-School Context

Students had been learning to write within an expository structure. They had written expository text for a variety of purposes, including grant applications and persuasive letters.

They had been learning about the structure of and purpose for writing editorials. Through classroom debates, students had taken a stand and defended their response to various "should" questions. One example was "Should students be rewarded for completing their homework?" Students had been learning that there is a difference between writing *about* a problem and writing *to solve* a problem. By reading various editorials, they concluded that identifying a problem is one of the first steps in writing an article that states an opinion or perspective. Students then read about kids who had improved their community by focusing on a problem; investigating it; and taking some course of action, which usually involved writing. The teacher modeled how to identify problems and emphasized their appearance in a variety of sources, including the media, daily conversations, and personal frustrations.

Inquiry Skills

- Ask questions.
- Identify problems.
- Choose sources and collect evidence.

Description of Assignment

- *Short-term:* Students located problems from a variety of sources to collect ideas for editorials. The teacher provided newspapers and a list of Web sites that presented current events at a grade-appropriate reading level. With their families, students located one problem at the local, state, national, or world level. Family members were encouraged to help each student find a problem that was of personal interest to him or her. They then discussed the problem by using the following questions:

  What are the causes of the problem?

  Who is affected by the problem?

  How might others feel about this problem, issue, or topic?

  Why should we care about the problem? Why does it need us?

  Which organization or professional sector is involved in solving the problem?

For the data collection tools that the students used in this assignment, see Appendix C.3.

- *Long-term:* Each student researched his or her problem and wrote statements to be used in surveys. These surveys helped students collect information about opinions throughout their community while building awareness of important issues. Students developed thesis statements and wrote editorials. They searched for organizations, nonprofits, and media outlets to serve as authentic audiences. The class also grouped the problems based on themes such as health, transportation, conflict, environment, money, etc. One theme became the focus for classroom study and a social action project.

Extensions

- Explore political cartoons as editorial statements.
- Use blogging as an editorial activity.

(Continued)

(Continued)

Cross Talk Questions

1. How can I help students to connect personally to major world problems? How can the teacher keep it "real" for the students?

   J.A. *Finding examples that involve children is one way. Another is breaking down a world problem example to illustrate what it might look like within our own community in the future. Relate it to actual individuals in the community. Invite local people into the classroom to discuss possible local implications.*

   B.B. *Chronicle how these issues impact kids from around the world.*

2. How can I help students understand that effective editorial writing is based on personal opinion combined with researched information?

   B.K. *Read many examples of editorials.*

   S.M. *Elicit feedback from audiences outside the classroom to learn how the editorial could be strengthened by using numbers, quotes, and facts.*

UPPER ELEMENTARY MATHEMATICS BEYOND METRIC CONVERSION

Principles of Meaningful Homework

- Providing for expanded meaningfulness and life application of school learning
- Constructing meaning in natural ways and expanding a sense of self-efficacy

National Standard

Measurement

Assignment Goal(s)

✓ Students will begin to understand the importance of the metric system as a common global language and examine the metric system transition process in the United States.

✓ Students will understand the many purposes for learning the metric system while investigating experiences that can increase the application of the metric system in their daily lives.

In-School Context

Students in a fifth-grade classroom had started a unit on measurement and learned about metric system units. They learned that almost every other country in the world uses the metric system and debated the following question: Should the citizens of the United States increase efforts to transition to the metric system?

Students had been researching difficulties involved with switching to the metric system and whether or not it would be in the country's best interest to overcome these difficulties.

They considered whether it is confusing that the United States uses a different measuring system than the rest of the world and looked into problems that may arise because of the use of different measuring systems. Students were starting to become aware of whether or not the metric system was used by medical professionals, the U.S. Postal Service, and NASA.

Students concluded as a class that the United States should make a greater effort to make the transition. The class brainstormed reasons why it has been so difficult for the United States to switch to the metric system and why it would be in the country's best interest to overcome these difficulties. Students were curious to find out why they had not become part of the worldwide metric environment. They wondered whether life experiences such as travel, family history, background in math or science, education, culture, and business practices had been factors contributing to their parents' (and, hence, their own) attitudes toward the metric system.

Inquiry Skills

- Collect and analyze data.
- Choose sources and collect evidence.
- Summarize findings and reflect.

Description of Assignment

- *Short-term:* Students conducted a survey of their families and community members in hopes of determining what people know about the metric system and how they felt about the ongoing conversion to metric. Students used a class-generated checklist to gather information on people's life experiences that may have contributed to their understanding of the metric system. Students then presented their rationale for conversion and responded to objections by those opposed to the conversion. Finally, they repeated the survey to see if attitudes had changed in favor of the metric system. They also drew conclusions about how people's life experiences impacted their willingness to convert. For the data collection tool that the students used in this assignment, see Appendix C.4.

- *Long-term:* Students talked to business and government officials about the implications of not converting to the metric system. They investigated the time- and money-saving aspects of using the metric system in manufacturing and the possible impact of conversion on U.S. exports and imports. Students also investigated U.S. laws such as the Metric Conversion Act (first passed in 1975 and still in effect). They gathered evidence on whether these laws are being enforced sufficiently and considered whether additional legislation would be to the advantage of the United States. At the local grocery store, they discussed with shoppers the advantages and disadvantages of metric conversion from the consumer's point of view, using questions such as the following: Why do you think it has been hard for the United States to switch to the metric system? Do you think it is in the country's best interest to overcome these difficulties? Do you think it is confusing that the United States uses a different measuring system than the rest of the world?

Extensions

- Discover business situations in which the metric system is used and explore the reasons why those businesses use the metric system (e.g., for communication or to gather more accurate data).

(Continued)

(Continued)

- Survey schools in other countries to find out what measurement system they study.
- Observe commonly used numbers in the local area and consider how they would change if the metric system were used (e.g., 75 mph speed limit would become 120 km/h).

Cross Talk Questions

1. How can I justify the time needed to complete this assignment when only a few math standards directly connect to the goal?

   J.A. *I think you are ahead of the curve. Metrics is the wave of the future! I think more standards will be allocated to it in the future.*

   B.B. *This could be an area of the curriculum in which the students' inquiry skills are emphasized (as opposed to content goals). Perhaps this assignment could be near the beginning of the year so as to make it serve both the academic goal and the skills development process, which could be built off it in the future.*

   B.K. *Think about and connect to other standards and to other areas, such as social studies and language arts (Persuasive Writing).*

2. How can I use this opportunity to clear up students' questions and confusion related to the metric system?

   S.M. *This assignment will allow you to see what misconceptions arise and give you a basis for instructional decisions.*

3. Will parents be willing to allow their children to speak with strangers?

   B.K. *Clarify with parents up front how this will be structured and how students would and/or should be supervised and supported.*

   S.M. *Parents could also take their children around their own neighborhood to speak with familiar adults.*

UPPER ELEMENTARY ART
ARTISTIC VISIONARIES FOR A BETTER FUTURE

Principles of Meaningful Homework

- Taking advantage of the students' diversity by using it as a learning resource
- Personalizing the curriculum and reflecting on the here and now

National Standard

Choosing and evaluating a range of subject matter, symbols, and ideas

Assignment Goal(s)

✓ Students will select and apply subject matter, symbols, and ideas to communicate meaning and understand how personal experiences can influence the development of artwork.

✓ Students will appreciate how visual arts have inherent relationships to everyday life and identify connections between the visual arts and contemporary issues and local concerns.
✓ Students will apply a sense of connectedness with the world and constructively express their hopes for change and social improvement.

In-School Context

Students in a multiaged class had been exploring contemporary social, cultural, and political issues through the visual arts. They had generated a list of questions or concerns that they had about themselves and the world in the future (Beane, 1997). Then they connected their personal and collective concerns to specific social issues such as sustainability, poverty, discrimination, technology, diversity, and conflict. Students learned that art could be used for different purposes, including connecting people through common social concerns. They studied works of art that attempted both to raise awareness and to persuade others to consider issues and their possible solutions. They also learned about diverse beliefs related to how these issues could be resolved in their community. All of their classroom learning focused on answering the following questions: How can our art influence the future? How can we use our art to impact our community positively?

Inquiry Skills

• Identify problems.
• Make observations.

Description of Assignment

• *Short-term:* Students investigated symbols, images, and ideas related to their social concern or issue. They applied observation strategies and created images from their everyday lives by taking photographs, making sketches, or using images in magazines and newspapers. These images expressed students' concerns for the future of their community. Students discussed with a family member how their images connected to their concerns. To enhance discussion about their images and distinguish their art aesthetically with their family, students used a list of adjectives and selected words that best described their art. Words such as *symmetrical, flowing, lively, hectic, calming, serious, lighthearted,* and *elegant* were used to enhance their explanations. Students shared these images in class and integrated them into artistic products. For the data collection tool that the students used in this assignment, see Appendix C.5.

• *Long-term:* Students interviewed community members to get their perspectives on the issues that they researched. After collecting and analyzing local data, they presented their family and community members with predictions for the next half century. Their presentations outlined emerging patterns and developments in health care, technology, the economy, media, and business. The class studied community artists and the processes they used to integrate their community's perspectives on local issues. Students then collaborated with a local artist to combine their art and their ideas for the future into a community mural. A final exhibition was held for the students to present their hopes and concerns for the future, where they defended their speculations with research collected from the community.

(Continued)

(Continued)

Extensions

- The class may be able to identify a schoolwide issue and then create an art display that challenges some aspect of the issue. Perhaps temporary murals, photos, or sculptures could be displayed throughout the building or even elsewhere on the school grounds.
- Students could take a field trip to a relevant art exhibit.
- Students could write to a politician to elicit his or her point of view and invite the politician to the school to see the art.

Cross Talk Questions

1. How will I engage parents who are hesitant about their child learning about social, political, and cultural issues?

   J.A. *Always have an open-door policy. In meeting with families early in the year, explain how you want to address touchy issues and why. Walk them through a lesson that is laced with concrete examples.*

   B.B. *Explain to families that people's ideas and beliefs about the world typically change over time. Furthermore, the ability to understand these issues from multiple perspectives is an important ability to develop.*

   B.K. *Offer time to share an upcoming unit or assignment with families. Set a time to share materials and resources needed to complete the assignment. By offering the open house, you create a feeling of openness with the curriculum.*

2. How can parents be equipped to assist their child in learning about difficult and sometimes depressing social issues?

   B.B. *It is important for learners of this age to begin to understand that life is often unfair. But parents should be encouraged to tell children that they don't just have to accept unfair situations, that they can affect positive change if they are willing to commit themselves to a particular cause.*

   B.K. *Model for parents possible responses to use when the students come home after critical class discussions.*

REFERENCES

Beane, J. (1997). *Curriculum integration: Designing the core of democratic education.* New York: Teachers College Press.

9

How Can Meaningful Homework Look in Middle School?

Sarah Middlestead

WHY IS MEANINGFUL HOMEWORK IMPORTANT TO THE MIDDLE SCHOOL LEARNER?

The middle school student faces many challenges that are unique to this stage of life. Peer pressure takes on a new meaning, and hormonal changes wreak havoc. Students have multiple teachers, maybe for the first time. Instead of a self-contained classroom, they are in departmentalized classes. This shift in the structure of the school day can allow many students to begin just going through the motions of school. It becomes easier to sit in the back of class and do just the minimal requirements. In some cases, students fall through the cracks and even go unnoticed for an entire day. Middle school students in particular are in danger of finding school meaningless, with no relevance to their lives.

"Why do I have to do this?" "When will I ever use this?" Middle school teachers hear these questions on a regular basis. As students enter young adulthood, they begin to determine what is useful and what is not. Students want to know that school tasks have some value, some sort of meaning. Questions may begin to surface when a teacher assigns countless math problems, a pile of worksheets, or any other rote activity. Practice has its place, but middle school students are reluctant to complete homework that does not serve a real purpose. They need to see that the work they are doing has meaning, that it connects to the real world, and that what they are learning actually matters in life and will be used as they enter adulthood. Meaningful homework makes explicit the connections between classroom content and the real world. Students are able to see that what they are doing in school matters to their lives in the here and now, causing them to ask "Why do I have to do this?" and "When will I ever use this?" much less frequently. In essence, meaningful homework answers these questions. In turn, this builds middle school students' self-efficacy, allowing them to develop the confidence to use what they learn at school in the world around them.

Students at the middle school level, particularly those who are at risk of failure and dropout, are at a crossroads. They are making decisions that will alter their educational future. Questions that students confront at the middle school level include the following: Will I take my education seriously? Does education have anything to offer me? Will I just "do school," or will I try to actually learn? Will I go on and graduate from high school, or will I drop out? Meaningful homework has the potential to sway students who are "on the fence" so that they give the right answers to these questions. As they begin to see that what is learned in school does apply to the world around them, they find new meaning and value in education. Those who just go through the motions of "doing school," and even those who are considering dropping out of school, will begin to see that learning is something of value.

EXTENDED EXAMPLE: MIDDLE SCHOOL MATHEMATICS—THE PATTERNS AROUND US

Principles of Meaningful Homework

- Constructing meaning in natural ways and expanding a sense of self-efficacy
- Personalizing the curriculum and reflecting on the here and now

National Standard

Representation

Assignment Goal(s)

✓ Students will understand how to represent, analyze, and generalize a variety of patterns.
✓ Students will know how to communicate their mathematical thinking effectively to peers, teachers, and others.
✓ Students will appreciate the mathematics present in the surrounding world, thereby increasing their mathematical self-efficacy.

In-School Context

In a unit entitled "From Patterns to Algebra," eighth-grade mathematics students have completed a review of the algebraic order of operations, variables, and evaluating expressions. This was the first unit of the year, so many students had not thought about mathematical concepts in quite some time and many showed reluctance to study mathematics again. Once students were firmly grounded in these foundational mathematical concepts, the class then proceeded to study number patterns, specifically focusing on identifying and extending numerical patterns. Knowing that a high percentage of students were struggling and at risk of failure, the teacher wanted to design a homework assignment that students would complete with a high rate of success, thereby increasing their self-efficacy in mathematics. In addition, the teacher wanted students to see that mathematics surrounds them in the world outside of school and that the concepts learned in school have a place in real life.

Inquiry Skills

- Collect and analyze data.
- Make observations.
- Choose sources and collect evidence.

Description of Assignment

For this task, students were given a disposable camera and instructed to take four pictures of patterns found outside of school. They could work independently or with a partner. Since there were only three disposable cameras per class, students took cameras home and brought them back the next day over two weeks.

Once every student had taken pictures, the film was developed and then uploaded to an online photography site. Using this site, the teacher and students collaboratively composed a book of the pattern pictures in which each picture was given a title and caption. Upon its completion, the book was donated to a first-grade class as a resource for their study of patterns. The eighth graders invited the first graders to come to their classroom for the presentation of the final product. Students from the two classes read the book together and talked about the patterns they discovered.

The value of this task was completely intrinsic for students, so the assignment was not graded in the traditional sense. Students took great pride in the pictures they took and an even greater pride in seeing them in a published book. The true feedback students received consisted of watching the first graders read the book they wrote. The eighth graders beamed with pride as they watched the first graders trying to determine the patterns in their pictures. In addition, for the rest of the year, students continually reported to the teacher the numerous patterns that they were seeing around them. Through this assignment, students realized that the things learned in mathematics are not limited to the classroom. Patterns are everywhere, and that is a foundational theme of algebraic concepts. For the data collection tool that the students used in this assignment, see Appendix D.1.

Cross Talk Questions

1. In an era of tight budgets, where can I find the funds to purchase disposable cameras, develop the film, and compose a book?

    B.B. *Digital cameras may be a solution. The final product could also be digital and e-mailed to the partnering lower elementary classroom. Otherwise, you may be able to find a local store that is willing to donate the film, film processing, etc.*

    J.A. *Sources of funds could be service clubs (e.g., Rotary), an individual donor, school system foundation, or a mini grant. In addition, students could collect recyclables to generate funds.*

    B.K. *Local photo studios could be asked to donate their services. You could also approach the company that takes your school pictures to see if it might donate cameras or film.*

(Continued)

(Continued)

2. How do I ensure that students take school-appropriate pictures, don't lose the camera, bring it back on time, don't damage it, etc.?

B.K.   *One student per class could be responsible for the camera. This student would sign the camera in and out and remind students to bring it back. Students could also sign a class agreement about the appropriate use of the camera.*

J.A.   *As a class, co-construct a list of guidelines for appropriate use of the camera. Make students responsible in as many aspects as possible.*

R.L.   *Have students share their photographs with a parent and get feedback.*

3. Students are just taking pictures! Does this homework assignment really impact students' mathematical self-efficacy?

B.B.   *Yes, by providing them with a meaningful and informative opportunity to be successful. The goals of this assignment have to be very clear to both students and parents.*

B.K.   *You could design and implement a preassessment of skills and attitudes and then compare the results to a post-assessment.*

MIDDLE SCHOOL SCIENCE
REDUCING YOUR CARBON FOOTPRINT

Principles of Meaningful Homework

- Providing for expanded meaningfulness and life application of school learning
- Extending education to the home and community by engaging adults in interesting and responsible ways

National Standard

Earth and Space Science

Assignment Goal(s)

✓ Students will appreciate that their daily actions make an impact on the earth.
✓ Students will understand how technology used in their daily lives impacts the surface of the earth.
✓ Students will apply scientific knowledge to work with their families in making a more positive impact on the earth.

In-School Context

Students in a middle school science class were studying the geosphere, including how rocks are formed, how rocks are broken down, how soil is formed, and how technology changes the surface of the earth. They were challenged to consider how the daily lifestyle of their family affects the geosphere.

Inquiry Skills

- Identify problems.
- Make observations.
- Summarize findings and reflect.

Description of Assignment

- *Short-term:* Students gathered information needed to calculate the carbon footprint of their family. This included amounts of energy used in the home, flights taken, transportation usage (car, motorbike, bus, and rail), eating habits, recycling, recreation, etc. Students put the collected information into an online carbon footprint calculator (www.carbonfootprint.com/calculator.aspx) to determine the carbon footprint of their family. For the data collection tool that the students used in this assignment, see Appendix D.2.

- *Long-term:* During the following weeks, students discussed with their families practical ways to reduce their carbon footprint and kept a journal together that detailed the changes that their families were making. Data were collected and put into the online carbon footprint calculator again to see if each family's carbon footprint had decreased. Students then hosted a Family Science Night in which families shared the ways in which they had made their impact on the earth more positive.

Extensions

- Contact local utilities to see about "green" programs.
- Look into Green School Certification.
- Ask students to weigh the trash that is generated in the cafeteria for a week, then focus on ways to reduce that waste and encourage their school to do the same. Later, they could weigh the trash again to see if improvement has occurred.

Cross Talk Questions

1. How do I link families' carbon footprints with the changing surface of the earth?

    B.B.　*Emphasize the collective nature of the impact on the earth.*

    B.K.　*Use your own family as a model and example. Keep coming back to this same concept in subsequent lessons.*

    J.A.　*Use your own footprint and recruit other teachers and the principal as points of departure. Recruit family volunteers to serve as examples. Also, use concrete examples to show hypothetical impacts of differing lifestyles on the earth.*

2. How can I generate enough excitement to bring families together for a Family Science Night? Will people actually come?

    B.K.　*Give each student a specific role to play or task to complete during the Family Science Night. This night could be run in an open-house style so that families are not restricted to attending at a specific time. In addition, students could make items ahead of time out of reusable materials and then give these items as favors during the evening.*

(Continued)

(Continued)

J.A. *Dare to try! Dare to do! Don't expect 100 percent attendance the first time. Word will spread when the experience is positive. Recruit key family volunteers to help recruit other people to attend. Have students generate a list of activities to be completed through the night with their family.*

B.B. *One way is by offering food! Also, have your students express the importance of this issue to their family members.*

3. What if families are not interested in reducing their carbon footprints?

R.L. *Have students share tips on how to convince their families of the benefits of reducing their carbon footprints.*

B.K. *Emphasize to students that they are not learning this just for today but for their own futures. Even if their own family is not interested, they will have the opportunity to decide for themselves as they become adults. Students can also focus on the things that they can control now, like turning off lights or taking shorter showers.*

B.B. *This runs contrary to current public opinion, but if there are easy and cost-saving ways to reduce their carbon footprints, many people will be willing to consider them (at least in a theoretical sense).*

MIDDLE SCHOOL SOCIAL STUDIES
BUILDING A CASE FOR THE FINE ARTS

Principles of Meaningful Homework

- Extending education to the home and community by engaging adults in interesting and responsible ways
- Personalizing the curriculum and reflecting on the here and now
- Exploiting learning opportunities that are not cost-effective on school time

National Standard

Power, Authority, and Governance

Assignment Goal(s)

✓ Students will know how people create and change structures of power, authority, and governance.
✓ Students will understand how power, authority, and governance apply at the school board level.
✓ Students will appreciate their own role in effecting change in policymaking.

In-School Context

Students in a middle school social studies class had been studying communities and local school governance. They had been informed that the fine arts program for Grades 5–12 would be affected by this decision, so they were anxious to talk about it. With encouragement from the principal, the teacher invited a school board member to the class to address questions that the students had generated.

Inquiry Skills

- Collect and analyze data.
- Summarize findings and reflect.

Description of Assignment

- Short-term: Students spoke to at least two neighborhood adults about the proposal to suspend the fine arts program for Grades 5–12. Questions included the following: What is your reaction? What do you view as alternatives or consequences? Students then brought a one-page written summary of their findings to school and were prepared to share these findings with the class. For the data collection tool that the students used in this assignment, see Appendix D.3.

- *Long-term: In the following weeks, students surveyed family and community members to determine their views regarding the school board's proposed actions, including alternatives to and potential consequences of such actions. Through these discussions, students elicited suggestions of alternatives, such as cutting back other programs, raising money to save the program, or generating a special assessment to offset the deficit. After gathering and analyzing the data, the class prepared a statement for the school board's consideration. A representative group from the class then presented the class recommendations to the school board.*

Extensions

- Look at past practices of the district with regard to similar problems or situations.
- Look at the school district's budget. How is money allocated?
- Compare to how families make budgetary decisions.
- Design an art exhibit that advocates for the arts entitled "Art About Art."
- Interview former art teachers about changes in programming and art education.

Cross Talk Questions

1. Should the students spend in-school time, prior to assigning this homework, talking about the purpose of school boards and how their powers are acquired, used, and justified?

   R.L. *Yes, after an initial interest-generating activity such as a role-play. You could start by interviewing school board members, tracking school board elections, discussing how decisions impact the school, or watching a school board meeting on television.*

   J.A. *This will be essential. Students often have family members, neighbors, or family friends who serve on school boards. They could be in-class resources. Obviously, you will need to prepare students for these discussions.*

2. How do you get support from your administrators to promote open lines of communication with school board members when they seem to fear the policymakers themselves?

   B.K. *Inform your administration from the beginning of your plans and goals for the assignment.*

(Continued)

(Continued)

R.L.   *Garner student and parent support before going to the principal.*

J.A.   *Make sure the administration has a clear grasp of your instructional goals and the major understandings you want your students to develop.*

3. How can I promote the credibility of the "student voice" in my community?

J.A.   *Build the norm in your district that students do have a viable voice. This takes time and lots of guidance on your part. Make sure the goals are explicit. Establish "safe" guidelines for students. Give students opportunities to learn the skills of persuasion and of reading an audience. Give them tools that foster credibility and voice.*

B.K.   *Be mindful of student writing you pass on to the public. Closely monitor the writing process and make sure that pieces used are good examples.*

4. What if no such issue presents itself in my school?

B.K.   *Analyze a situation from the recent past and discuss what could have been done. You could also use public records to look into situations from nearby school districts.*

J.A.   *Anticipate a move in the future that will require cost cutting. Discuss the best- and worst-case scenarios.*

R.L.   *Involve students in finding a problem. Prior to starting the assignment, generate a list of their ideas.*

MIDDLE SCHOOL ENGLISH LANGUAGE ARTS
WAR THROUGH THE GENERATIONS

Principles of Meaningful Homework

- Extending education to the home and community by engaging adults in interesting and responsible ways
- Taking advantage of the students' diversity by using it as a learning resource

National Standard

Students read a wide range of literature from many periods in many genres to build an understanding of the many dimensions (e.g., philosophical, ethical, aesthetic) of human experience.

Assignment Goal(s)

✓ Students will read and understand three books from different time periods and genres, comparing and contrasting themes that emerge.
✓ Students will apply content from the books in meaningful discussions with people of different generations.
✓ Students will apply their own perspectives and those of people they know to the reading of required texts.

In-School Context

Students in a middle school language arts class read *My Brother Sam Is Dead* by James and Christopher Collier (American Revolutionary War; 1974), *The Foreshadowing* by Marcus Sedgwick (World War I; 2006), and *Night* by Elie Wiesel (World War II; 1960). Each of these three books, from different time periods and different genres, addresses the topic of war. Students compared the perceptions of war from the three books and were then asked to see if their observations held true for real human experience.

Inquiry Skills

- Collect and analyze data.
- Summarize findings and reflect.

Description of Assignment

- *Short-term*: Students spoke with at least three people about the subject of war: a grandparent, a parent, and a peer. If one of these people was not available, the student could choose someone else of a similar age. Prior to the interviews, students anticipated what they might hear from people of different generations. Interview questions included the following: What memories of war do you have? How has war affected you personally? For the data collection tool that the students used in this assignment, see Appendix D.4.

- *Long-term:* Students read excerpts from one of the books with each of the three people they originally interviewed. Discussion questions included the following: Does the excerpt match your perspective of war? What new thoughts does it bring to mind? Data from the original interview and the book-excerpt discussions were then discussed as a whole class. What patterns emerged? Do people of the same generation feel the same about war? Do themes cross generational lines? It was then discussed how being engaged in the true human experience of war enriches the reading of classroom texts.

Extensions

- Find primary historical sources for these three eras and compare them to the books.
- Ask students to decide in which generation they would most prefer to live and defend their choice.

Cross Talk Questions

1. Do I have enough time to read three books with my students and then do these assignments? What about the rest of my curriculum?

   B.K.   *You could use excerpts as opposed to the whole text.*

   R.L.   *Structure book clubs and then have students report back to the whole class. In this way, students learn about all of the texts but do not have to read them all.*

2. Some or all of these books are not on my district's book list. Can I still have my students read them?

   BB: *Check into your district's policy regarding book lists. Could there be a way to read additional books that are not on the book list?*

(Continued)

(Continued)

BK: *Compare the books you have chosen to the ones on your district's list. Be prepared to discuss adding the books you have chosen to that list. Be clear about your rationale for choosing these books and be ready to articulate it.*

3. What if students cannot find three generations of people to interview?

BK: *Use adults within the school community. Have "interview teams" of three students interview one adult. Have students work in groups to cover all of the needed generations so that not every student has to interview someone in every generation.*

JA: *Focus on one generation and report back to the class. In this way, students do not have to interview individuals from all three generations.*

MIDDLE SCHOOL PHYSICAL EDUCATION
THE MEDIA'S IMPACT ON PHYSICAL HEALTH

Principles of Meaningful Homework

- Providing for expanded meaningfulness and life application of school learning
- Constructing meaning in natural ways and expanding a sense of self-efficacy
- Personalizing the curriculum and reflecting on the here and now

National Standard

Participates in regular physical activity.

Assignment Goal(s)

✓ Students will look critically at media propaganda and appreciate the impact that it makes on adolescent society.
✓ Students will understand the benefits of physical activity and become more physically active.

In-School Context

Students in a middle school physical education classroom studied why it is important to be involved in regular physical activity. After looking at the physical, mental, and emotional benefits of being physically active, they were challenged to look critically at how society and the media either encourage or discourage teenagers to be physically healthy.

Inquiry Skills

- Ask questions.
- Choose sources and collect evidence.

Description of Assignment

- *Short-term:* Students designed a survey as a class that would elicit opinions about the media and physical health. Students predicted what the data would show and then surveyed people outside of school. For the data collection tool that the students used in this assignment, see Appendix D.5.

- *Long-term:* Students compiled the data as a class and graphed the results. Over the next couple of weeks, they searched the media for examples of teenagers being encouraged or discouraged to be physically active. Data were compiled as a class, and emerging trends were discussed. Discussion questions included the following: Do students feel that society and the media generally help teenagers to be healthy? Do the results of their media searches match what they had predicted? Students then designed their own advertisements that encouraged teenagers to engage in regular physical activity. These student-generated ads were compiled so that students could launch an ad campaign schoolwide.

Extensions

- Contact local businesses and see how they advertise, promote, and connect with families.
- Complete a cost analysis of local options for physical health.

Cross Talk Questions

1. How can I ensure the media sources used will be appropriate for school?

   R.L. *Involve parents! If students have to show material to their parents, they may be less likely to choose something questionable.*

   B.B. *Use one of many teacher tools (e.g., Delicious and PortaPortal) to monitor Web sites that are used.*

2. What if my students just do not care about being physically active?

   J.A. *Unfortunately, there will be students who are totally uninterested in this topic at the outset. Yet they need exposure to issues associated with teenage health. Elicit testimonials from adults they admire. Find places in your community that promote fitness.*

   B.K. *As a preassessment, survey students to find their interests. To motivate interest, you could also have students share publicly.*

   R.L. *Connect this activity to instruction. Try to encourage new settings for physical activity and make it social. Get students outside. Have them design new games and schedule optional activities such as laser tag.*

3. Will topics be presented that I might not be comfortable discussing with my students? How would I handle this?

   J.A. *Literature or video might be a means to present neutral positions, and they typically have clear explanations.*

   B.K. *List these issues ahead of time and plan how to approach them should they be presented in class. Rehearse your responses.*

REFERENCES

Collier, J., & Collier, C. (1974). *My brother Sam is dead.* New York: Four Winds Press.

Sedgwick, M. (2006). *The foreshadowing.* New York: Wendy Lamb Books.

Wiesel, E. (1960). *Night.* New York: Hill and Wang.

10

How Can Meaningful Homework Look in High School?

Ben Botwinski

WHY IS MEANINGFUL HOMEWORK IMPORTANT TO THE HIGH SCHOOL LEARNER?

High school students' proximity to adulthood is the first important consideration. Adolescence is defined as the period between puberty and maturity, a time when young people acquire their adult identities and begin to think and behave as adults. Homework should reflect this evolving self-perception. Meaningful homework grounded in the real-world application of knowledge and skills is usually perceived as having greater relevance and purpose than rote assignments. If teachers can design homework that embodies these characteristics, students may be more likely to engage in the work and gain from the effort and energy spent.

A second important consideration is that students enter high school with firmly established habits and practices related to homework—a "homework identity." Parents and families of these learners often are acutely aware of this identity and, inadvertently, perpetuate the associated behaviors (both positive and negative). Teachers need to be mindful of these identities in order to encourage positive change in student habits and practices. Through meaningful homework, teachers, students, and families can engage in renewed dialogue about purposes and expectations related to homework.

The third reason why meaningful homework is so important to high school learners has nothing to do with adolescent development or psychology. Rather, it has to do with the perceptions and behaviors of parents. Research indicates that as a student progresses through the K–12 system, parental involvement tends to diminish—especially in regards to academics. As a result, the divide between home and school is magnified, and ultimately learning suffers. By providing students and their parents with opportunities to engage with the curriculum, meaningful homework can minimize the distance between the classroom and the living room.

EXTENDED EXAMPLE: HIGH SCHOOL SOCIAL STUDIES WEIGHING RIGHTS AND RESPONSIBILITIES

Principles of Meaningful Homework

- Providing for expanded meaningfulness and life application of school learning
- Constructing meaning in natural ways and expanding a sense of self-efficacy
- Extending education to the home and community by engaging adults in interesting and responsible ways

National Standard

Power, Authority, and Governance

Assignment Goal(s)

✓ Students will collect information about how the relationship between individual rights and civic responsibilities plays out in immediate family and community situations.
✓ Students will engage in meaningful classroom discourse through the introduction of multiple and diverse perspectives related to complex social challenges.
✓ Students will employ the findings in a reference resource for the unit assessment.

In-School Context

Ensuring that students have a strong understanding of the structures and roles of government in modern American society, as well as in other areas of the world, is essential for fostering civic competence. In this ninth-grade social studies class, exploration of civic concepts began with a unit in which students examined the underlying ideologies and characteristics of diverse governance systems. One specific area of comparison between systems was the relationship between individual rights and civic responsibilities. In exploring the relationship between rights and responsibilities, learners became more aware of the concept of a "just society" and were better able to understand the multidimensional nature of persistent social challenges facing modern America. Nested within this unit were several lessons designed to provide learners with opportunities to apply their knowledge, experience, and skills toward potential solutions to one of America's persistent social challenges. The following example of meaningful homework was grounded in this context.

Inquiry Skills

- Ask questions.
- Collect and analyze data.
- Summarize findings and reflect.

(Continued)

(Continued)

Description of Assignment

This assignment provided a natural mechanism for nurturing intergenerational communication by encouraging students to share and discuss what they were learning in school with their families. The idea was to use homework to provide a forum for interaction, not to suggest that families were to "teach" what was not accomplished in school. The assignment encouraged students to talk about what they were learning with their families and fostered a more active role in the learning process. In this way, the learning became more meaningful and personally relevant than it would have been otherwise.

The questions that students were to discuss with adults were meant to elicit the opinions and ideas that individuals held in relation to general social studies concepts and ideas. For example, parents were asked to share their opinions about immigration or stem cell research and provide their child with some rationale for that opinion. In return, their child was expected to share his or her opinions and rationales. Students were typically given four to six questions to discuss with their parents over one week. Questions were related to broad themes being discussed in class (e.g., individual rights and civic responsibilities). The exchange with their parents was to be recorded by students and then shared with the class in order to enrich classroom dialogue.

After initially explaining the premise of the assignment to students, the teacher would invite a colleague into class and model the expected interactions and behaviors. Then the students would practice discussing these questions with a partner so the two-way exchange of ideas would become more familiar to them and they could assess their own strengths and weaknesses. The teacher would then finish the explanation of the assignment by reviewing the guidelines and expectations, reinforcing the fact that the ideas exchanged would ultimately enhance the classroom community's understanding of these complex social challenges by providing different perspectives and opinions.

On the day the assignment was turned in, the teacher began class by asking students to share salient findings related to their discussions from the past week. Usually a few really excited students would be willing to share, and the ideas and opinions expressed during this time would launch the class into the day's lesson. Throughout the remainder of the class, the teacher provided opportunities for students to share relevant ideas expressed during the preceding discussions, thus adding substance to their continued exploration of the relationship between individual rights and civic responsibilities.

At the end of class, after everyone who wanted to share had the opportunity and assignments were collected, the teacher would compile a list of the findings and provide a copy for students to keep in their notes. Often the writing portion of their unit assessment would require students to take a stance on a particular issue and support it with sound reasoning and examples. The data gathered from these interactive assignments were particularly helpful in providing students with a starting point for the completion of the writing piece of the unit assessment. Another strategy used for informally assessing the degree to which these homework assignments actually enhanced classroom discourse was for the teacher to keep a copy of seating chart (or classroom roster) nearby throughout the lesson. Each time a student contributed to the discussion, the teacher would put a mark next to his or her name. The teacher would then compare the number of students who contributed to class when these assignments were completed to the number of students that contributed to class when these assignments were not part of the lesson. For the data collection tool that the students used in this assignment, see Appendix E.1.

Cross Talk Questions

1. How would I grade these types of interactive assignments?

    S.M. *Try not grading them. You may encounter some resistance, so a credit/no-credit system might be an alternative.*

    R.L. *Explore alternative forms of grading (such as the Socratic way) based on levels of conversation and student contribution to class discussion.*

    J.A. *Co-construct a rubric with students that would allow for self, peer, and parent grading.*

2. What if a parent simply refused, or was unable, to participate in conversations with their child?

    S.M. *Use the human resources that exist in the school or in the community at large, such as school board members, school staff, and supportive community members.*

    R.L. *Address participation before the assignment goes home. Parents should be the first option. A teacher could also post a video of a parent and child engaging in this assignment on the class Web site in order to lessen any anxiety.*

    B.K. *Allow students who need a substitute to suggest or propose an alternate. Try not to assign them to a complete stranger.*

3. Many parents and their children are already having these types of discussions, so what purpose does it serve to force the issue?

    J.A. *Embrace the fact that this is going on, and let parents know that we would like their children to be able to bring that information into the classroom.*

    B.K. *Explain that these assignments provide a structured, shared experience that creates a foundation for further communication.*

HIGH SCHOOL SCIENCE
ENVIRONMENTAL APPLICATION OF ACTIVATION ENERGY

Principles of Meaningful Homework

- Providing for expanded meaningfulness and life application of school learning
- Personalizing the curriculum and reflecting on the here and now
- Exploiting learning opportunities that are not cost-effective on school time

National Standard

Physical Science

Assignment Goal(s)

✓ Students will better understand the everyday applications of activation energy.
✓ Students will understand the relationship between activation energy and energy efficiency.

(Continued)

(Continued)

In-School Context

Students in a high school physical science or chemistry class were studying energy and rates in chemical reactions, including topics such as combustion, thermochemistry, and Hess's law. In the following example, students were introduced to concepts such as collision theory, Maxwell-Boltzman distribution, and activation energy. Students were then asked to consider how the rate of a chemical reaction is dependent upon temperature and activation energy.

Inquiry Skills:

- Collect and analyze data.
- Make observations.
- Choose sources and collect evidence.

Description of Assignment

- *Short-term:* Students were asked to identify at least five different areas or items in their homes in which the concept of activation energy was important (e.g., light bulbs, cooking/stoves, matches, fuel in vehicles, food decomposition and refrigeration, etc.). After gathering this information, they were asked to describe the reactions and speculate as to the level of activation energy required. For the data collection tool that the students used in this assignment, see Appendix E.2.

- *Long-term:* Using examples drawn from the short-term assignment, students were to complete a report on one particular situation in which activation energy was important. For example, one student wrote about how activation energy was important in terms of the creation of safe and renewable forms of fuels. Another student wrote about how energy-efficient appliances reduced the minimum threshold of activation energy needed to perform an intended function and thus saved on energy usage and costs. To increase their academic rigor, these reports could have been more technical and could have included actual descriptions of chemical reactions.

Extensions

- Compare/contrast "green" appliances.
- Design ads for "green" appliances that depict the concept of activation energy.
- Design and possibly build inventions related to activation energy.
- Write a children's book depicting key concepts and travel to an elementary school to share.
- Tap a series of ads to see which energy-efficient products people are most interested in.

Cross Talk Questions

1. While I think that this assignment has practical merit, it also seems fairly easy and has little relevance to the kinds of information that students at the high school level are expected to know about chemistry. How could it be modified to make it more rigorous and intellectually demanding?

    S.M.   *Highlight the math. This assignment could be taught in collaboration with a mathematics teacher in such a way that the mathematics of physical science and chemistry is highlighted.*

R.L.   *Connect it to the long-term assignment as a way to strengthen the rigor. Explain and make clear the overall purpose of the assignment and encourage students to make their initial observations robust.*

J.A.   *Talk with a family member or friend interested in creating new innovations. Ask the students how they would make the assignment more challenging.*

2. The location in which I am teaching is rife with manufacturers and engineers who, I assume, are mindful of the concept of activation energy. In what ways could I employ these local assets in order to raise my students' understanding of this interesting scientific concept?

S.M.   *Invite manufacturers and engineers into the classroom to share their practical knowledge of activation energy. In addition, students could interview or even shadow these professionals in the workplace. Students might even videotape their interviews or experiences in the field and then bring the tapes back to share with their classmates.*

J.A.   *Contact a local organization for engineers. Interview family members who might have specialized knowledge.*

B.K.   *Contact local trade unions for industry references.*

3. After the students gather the information or write the report, in what ways could the information be used to enrich classroom learning?

S.M.   *They could travel to other physical science or chemistry classrooms to share their learning. A Parents' Night could be structured in which students share findings with their families. Work could be printed in the school newspaper or broadcast on the school television station if one is available.*

B.K.   *Press the students to decide where to go next with the assignment and the learning they have gained.*

J.A.   *Display the work somewhere in the building. Invite professionals to be an authentic audience.*

HIGH SCHOOL MATHEMATICS
THE FUNCTION OF FUNCTIONS

Principles of Meaningful Homework

- Personalizing the curriculum and reflecting on the here and now
- Exploiting learning opportunities that are not cost-effective on school time

National Standard

Identify the family of functions best suited for modeling a given real-world situation. (1) Identify essential quantitative relationships and determine the class or classes of functions that might model them. (2) Use symbolic expressions, including iterative and recursive forms, to represent relationships arising from various contexts. (3) Draw reasonable conclusions about the situation being modeled.

(Continued)

(Continued)

Assignment Goal(s)

✓ Students will apply their knowledge of algebra to assess which professions commonly make use of mathematical functions.
✓ Students will gain a better understanding of real-world applications of functions.
✓ Students will familiarize themselves with a variety of potential professional avenues in which mathematics is used.

In-School Context

Students in a high school algebra class have been solving different algebraic functions (i.e., linear, quadratic, cubic, inverse, and odd/even functions). In the following example, students were asked to review real-world situations in which these functions present themselves. Students were then asked to identify the class of functions best suited for modeling a given real-world situation, use symbolic expressions to represent a given relationship, and draw a reasonable conclusion.

Inquiry Skills

- Collect and analyze data.
- Make observations.
- Choose sources and collect evidence.

Description of Assignment

- *Short-term:* Students were asked to identify three professions that regularly make use of algebraic functions and provide information about the types of functions typically used in each profession. They then were asked to provide one specific example of the use/application of a function by these professionals. For the data collection tool that the students used in this assignment, see Appendix E.3.

- *Long-term:* For those students who demonstrated interest, the teacher arranged a job-shadowing experience with a professional who used mathematical functions regularly. Students were asked to maintain a journal of their shadowing experience with this professional to be shared later with their peers. The professionals were also invited to speak to the class.

Extensions

- Build catapults, which demonstrate parabolic functions, and have professionals evaluate their design for mathematical proficiency.
- Visit a university and audit a class that trains professionals who use mathematics.
- Re-create an authentic product witnessed while job shadowing.
- Investigate algebraic concepts students may use in their own current jobs.

Cross Talk Questions

1. This type of assignment does not provide students with the opportunity to practice their mathematical skills. So how do I justify providing this experience at the expense of time spent practicing math?

R.L.   *Ask students to create math problems for their peers to solve. This could be used as an assessment of knowledge gained. By creating problems, students may gain understandings useful in solving problems.*

S.M.   *This activity builds a framework for students in which mathematics begins to make sense. Students see that the work they do in school has application to the world outside of the classroom. This shows students that mathematics has a purpose and thereby builds their self-efficacy.*

J.A.   *Assignments of this nature demonstrate for students the applicability of the knowledge gained.*

B.K.   *These assignments create a better understanding of why the content is taught.*

2. What if I live in an area where few professionals use mathematical functions regularly? How do I provide my students with this opportunity?

B.K.   *Use the Internet and library resources to find professionals who employ advanced mathematical knowledge.*

S.M.   *Emphasize that mathematics is foundational to many professions. Challenge students to dig deeper if their beginning claim is that math is not used in their area. If a more extensive search still is fruitless, students could take virtual field trips using Internet resources. Conference calls could be made in which students talk with a professional.*

J.A.   *Broaden your search to consider positions/professions that use mathematics in less traditional ways (e.g., building contractors).*

HIGH SCHOOL ENGLISH LANGUAGE ARTS CHARACTERS WANTED!

Principles of Meaningful Homework

- Providing for expanded meaningfulness and life application of school learning
- Extending education to the home and community by engaging adults in interesting and responsible ways
- Personalizing the curriculum and reflecting on the here and now

National Standard

Students adjust their use of spoken, written, and visual language (e.g., conventions, style, vocabulary) to communicate effectively with a variety of audiences and for different purposes.

Assignment Goal(s)

✓ Students will develop an understanding of the fact that different audiences exist and learn how to shape their writing to appeal most effectively to each audience.
✓ Students will review the differences between persuasive and informative forms of writing.
✓ Students will apply their understanding of the format of a business resume and cover letter.

(Continued)

(Continued)

In-School Context

Students in a high school English language arts class (World Literature) have been reading *Things Fall Apart* (Achebe, 1959), *Siddhartha* (Hesse, 1922), and *The Joy Luck Club* (Tan, 1989). In the following lesson, students reviewed or were introduced to the conventions, styles, and vocabulary associated with two distinct forms of written communication: informative and persuasive. They also reviewed the concept of an "audience" for their writing, identified various audiences, and discussed strategies for appealing to different audiences.

Inquiry Skills

- Collect and analyze data.
- Choose sources and collect evidence.

Description of Assignment

- *Short-term:* Students were asked to write a one-page letter to a family member persuading him or her to read one of the texts mentioned above. The letter reflected the salient points from the novel and employed the key concepts covered in class.

- *Long-term:* Students were asked to read classified ads and identify one position for which they were interested in submitting a resume. Then, from the perspective of one of the novel's protagonists, they were to compose a one-page resume. They also wrote a one-page cover letter in which they attempted to persuade a potential employer that they (as the protagonist) were suitable for the position. For the data collection tool that the students used in this assignment, see Appendix E.4.

Extensions

- Run mock job interviews in which students assume the personality of a character.
- Form book clubs.
- Provide an excerpt from the text and have the student and family write reviews of it and compare notes.
- Upload the reviews written by the students to a particular Web site.
- Use the reviews written by students in the school newspaper or library.
- Have students write letters to the school board about additions to the district's book list.
- Ask many students to apply for the same position and select finalists based on the quality of their resumes and cover letters.

Cross Talk Questions

1. In my district, we use a particular type of writing format and grading method. Could an assignment such as this be adapted to fit my district's writing policy?

    J.A.   *I am not sure that every assignment has to be adapted. But the reality is that students will be asked to write in certain ways. We may be doing students a disservice by not providing multiple formats for writing.*

    B.K.   *If you are going to deviate, be prepared to defend why this assignment needed to have different writing requirements.*

    R.L.   *Use the qualities of good writing to help demonstrate/justify its implementation.*

2. In my school, we have a career coordinator or counselor to help students prepare for life after high school. In what ways could I draw on this individual to increase the value of this assignment by strengthening my students' understanding of audience?

   B.K.   *Meet with the career coordinator to find out what work has already been completed and, if feasible, connect your teaching with this previous work.*

   J.A.   *Ask the career coordinator to invite professionals to be an authentic audience when students are presenting finished products.*

3. I already have quality assignments designed for many of my units, and our school policy states that what happens in one class (in terms of assignments) also has to happen in equivalent classes. How do I persuade my colleagues of the merit of such assignments?

   J.A.   *Meet the minimum requirements and then go beyond. Use the word* pilot *to give yourself some wiggle room. Be gutsy!*

   B.K.   *Convince your colleagues to let you try the assignment first in your classroom and then discuss its merits with them afterwards.*

   S.M.   *Begin by defining "quality" and making sure that the existing assignments maintain some aspects of meaningfulness. Rethink homework within a new framework of "quality."*

HIGH SCHOOL FOREIGN LANGUAGE
WHAT IS IN A WORD?

Principles of Meaningful Homework

- Extending education to the home and community by engaging adults in interesting and responsible ways
- Taking advantage of the students' diversity by using it as a learning resource
- Personalizing the curriculum and reflecting on the here and now

National Standard

Develop insight into the nature of language and culture.

Assignment Goal(s)

✓ Students will demonstrate an understanding of the nature of language through a comparison of the language being studied and their native language.
✓ Students will further develop their foreign language vocabulary and fluency.

In-School Context

Students in a high school foreign language classroom had been studying basic vocabulary and grammatical rules. As the "Around the Home" unit came to a close, the teacher asked students to begin thinking about the multiple ways in which the language being studied differed from their native language. The students were asked to brainstorm some of these differences, to speculate as to why those differences had developed, and finally to hypothesize about what such differences said about the respective cultures.

(Continued)

(Continued)

Inquiry Skills

- Ask questions.
- Collect and analyze data.
- Summarize findings and reflect.

Description of Assignment

- *Short-term:* The students selected one similarity between languages (e.g., tones, body language, common words, grammatical structures) and wrote a one-page paper that explored the origin of the similarity. The class then shared their findings and compiled a collective set of explanations, which was revisited after further language development. For the data collection tool that the students used in this assignment, see Appendix E.5.

- *Long-term:* Students interviewed a foreign-language speaker to explore similarities and differences that the speaker perceived between the two languages. The students' questions explored the origins of those similarities and differences, as well as what each similarity and difference said about the respective cultures. The key points of these interviews were shared in oral presentations.

Extensions

- Lobby for alternate foreign language offerings in your school.
- Invite representatives of professions in which foreign language skills are helpful (e.g., law enforcement, business, nursing).
- Travel to elementary schools in teams to teach basic foreign language lessons.
- Learn and discuss how languages acquire new words and expand their vocabulary.
- Study the derivations of words.
- Explore how English speakers are viewed in international settings.

Cross Talk Questions:

1. Do all the foreign language speakers to be interviewed in the long-term assignment have to speak the same language being studied by the students?

   J.A.   *If possible, start with speakers of the language being studied. Then move on to other foreign language speakers.*

2. Many of the students in my school are not native English speakers. How might this assignment be modified in order to draw on the diversity within my classroom?

   B.K.   *Know your students well. Find out what languages they already have access to and use them as assets.*

   R.L.   *Students could be grouped into teams made up of native English speakers and non–native English speakers. Each group could explore the differences they find among themselves.*

3. How might this assignment be modified for students with third- and fourth-year foreign language proficiencies?

   S.M.   *Consider switching the long-term and the short-term components. If the students conduct the interview first, the writing assignment would be more authentic and rigorous because they are writing from a base of real and personally discovered data.*

REFERENCES

Achebe, C. (1959). *Things fall apart.* New York: Anchor Books.

Hesse, H. (1922). *Siddhartha.* New York: Bantam Press.

Tan, A. (1989). *The joy luck club.* New York: Putnam

11

Still Not Convinced?

The intent of this chapter is to address questions that may still be on your mind about homework-related issues. The questions are divided into the following five categories:

1. Student challenges

2. Family challenges

3. Teacher challenges

4. Administrator challenges

5. School culture challenges

Questioning is healthy and productive as long as it is intended to seek better answers in the spirit of continuous improvement. Admittedly, homework will not solve all curricular or instructional problems; however, we view it as a powerful ingredient in the learning process. Ongoing attention to the multiple challenges is essential as we continue pursuing our goal to, someday, "get it right." Or at least almost!

STUDENT CHALLENGES

1. What does meaningful homework look like for learners who have special needs, such as learning disabilities?

Several qualities of meaningful homework support students with learning disabilities and other special needs. First, meaningful homework often encourages and even requires families to participate in the assignment. This becomes a built-in support mechanism for students with special needs as they work through the required steps. Family members often know exactly what kind of support their student needs. Secondly, working on inquiry skills as a classroom community before giving an assignment allows students to practice what they will need to be successful with the assignment. It also gives the teacher the opportunity to anticipate where a student might struggle. The teacher then can modify the assignment for that student before work on it begins.

Meaningful assignments often are adaptable to meet the needs of any student. Since meaningful assignments frequently do not have a single "right" answer, they allow students to feel confident and more successful. Also, teachers can work with family members and the special education staff to create an assignment that meets the goals for the teacher and supports the individual needs of the student. For example, if writing and recording information are difficult for a student, the teacher could interview the student and record the student's answers in written or tape-recorded form. The teacher could then have the special education teacher or a paraprofessional summarize the student's responses or transcribe the tape. That way, the student is much more likely to participate and complete the assignment.

To be successful with this type of support, the teacher needs to have clear goals and expectations for each assignment. Also, it is important to make certain that all students understand the assignment and all the work necessary to complete it before they begin. Teacher modeling, assignment organizers, direct instruction of skills, and clear expectations all work together to support students with learning disabilities who might otherwise struggle to be successful.

2. What does meaningful homework look like for students who are gifted learners?

Get to know gifted learners and how they think about homework assignments. Some gifted students struggle with traditional homework because of motivational factors, poor time management, or limited organizational proficiency. Homework should be optimally challenging for the gifted student. Homework that is not challenging or stimulating can be tedious, so gifted students may not complete it. On the other hand, homework that is too difficult can lead to anxiety. Create assignments that provide enough structure to make gifted students feel confident that they can complete them but that are also open-ended enough to allow gifted students to personalize the investigation and take the assignment as far as they can.

Especially at the secondary level, gifted students may be concerned about maintaining their grades and managing the amount of work that they put into each class. At this point in their schooling, they have become the most successful students at "doing school." They can be unwilling to step outside of the normal homework structure for fear that they may not receive a grade that will improve their GPA or prepare them for an advanced course. Try to shift their thinking and help them understand that these assignments are about more than just meeting the request of the teacher and satisfying a course requirement. Integrating their interests and concerns and channeling their work ethic into leadership roles empower gifted students to get more involved with meaningful homework assignments.

Using words such as *enrichment* helps students and families feel increased comfort with assignments that break from the traditional homework mold. Also, consider how you can most effectively communicate to gifted learners and their families the purposes of these assignments. Take time to explain how the assignments will prepare them for the present course of study and the future.

3. What does meaningful homework look like for learners who speak English as a second language?

Meaningful homework incorporates experiences that draw on students' homes and communities. With the appropriate level of support, meaningful homework can be beneficial to ELL students because it provides opportunities for language use in multiple settings and encourages students to assume increased responsibility for their learning. Each home-learning situation will place its unique demands on students and encourage wide-ranging types of language use and practice with English.

Through linkages among their homes, communities, and the classroom, students will come to see homework as an integral part of their lives and feel that their diverse backgrounds are honored and needed in the classroom. Meaningful homework provides an opportunity for ELL students to feel that their participation is valued. ELL students bring to the classroom firsthand knowledge of the customs, thoughts, and feelings of people in other cultures and sometimes other countries. Through the sharing of these resources, all students can benefit.

Most teachers already plan for the instruction of both ELL and English-proficient students as they organize their classroom activities. Some shifts in approach are necessary in regards to designing meaningful homework. However, the kinds of interventions that can be helpful to ELL students are the same ones that are effective for all students.

Sometimes ELL students need additional support to assist them in understanding the homework directions. In class, the teacher should model following the directions and using the skills needed to complete the homework. The teacher should also provide nonlinguistic examples, such as visual organizers, photographs, role-plays, and demonstrations, which can help to explain or clarify the content and objectives of the assignment.

In addition, the teacher should provide opportunities for ELL students to get started on their homework in class so that they can clarify any questions that they might have. This will prevent them from spending their time and energy at home trying to interpret the directions. If ELL students are given a long-term assignment, the teacher should check in with them frequently to monitor their progress and provide needed assistance.

ELL parents often feel isolated from school activities, so translating written material is essential. There are free online Web translators that teachers can use to translate directions into the ELL family's primary language. Homework opportunities requiring sustained dialogue and substantive language use should occur in the family's most fluent language. Older peers who have higher English proficiency can be used to support ELL students during all stages of the homework assignment.

4. I have students who will simply defy me, saying that since they are going to college all they care about is the test score. How can I encourage these students to complete and learn from meaningful homework assignments?

Explain to these students that a college education partially prepares them for a profession, but as college graduates, they will have to apply their learning in practical ways as they proceed into the workforce. Active participation in meaningful homework prepares students for the transition from college to the workforce, because it guides them in applying what they have learned in school to the world around them as they pursue their careers. Also explain to them that meaningful homework cements the concepts learned in the classroom. This will increase their understanding of and ability to apply those concepts, thereby having a positive impact on their test scores.

Meaningful homework gives students a chance to be active by interviewing, surveying, or talking with family and friends. Essentially, enthusiastic participation in meaningful homework enhances the student's learning. For the outright defiant student, the question really becomes "Why *wouldn't* you want to do this homework?"

5. My students will not do homework if I do not give a traditional grade. How can I handle this?

This is an immense challenge, because as students progress through the grades, they become ever more accustomed to typical classroom practices like the grading of assignments. In essence, they learn to "do school." Parents also become accustomed to their children "doing school," so the pressure to maintain the status quo is intense and changes to established practices are often perceived as radical.

However, teachers can make progress if they handle the situation with some finesse. Again, communication among all stakeholders is critical. When teachers talk about assigning tasks that will not be graded, what they are really saying is that they would like to change one particular aspect of the classroom culture. Changes such as these tend to go smoothly if they are timed so as to be aligned with a naturally occurring transition period, such as the beginning of the year, a new semester, or even a new unit.

Another important element is finding a way to motivate students without the extrinsic motivation of grades. It is worth mentioning that because an assignment is not going to be graded, it does not necessarily follow that the only source of motivation remaining is students' intrinsic motivation. There are multiple extrinsic ways other than grades to motivate students to complete their assignments. One key to unlocking these other forms of motivation is to understand the importance of the design and use of the homework. The design of the assignment and the use of the end product need to be reimagined as having purposes and outcomes other than grades.

The manner in which the assignment is used after it is completed is important. Teachers should ensure that there is a clear and immediate application of the product after the assignment is complete and should also try to broaden the audience that is exposed to or will use the product. Teachers should share student work with other students, parents, or community members who may be interested. In this way, teachers can motivate students to move their thinking beyond the specific grade associated with an assignment and toward an understanding of the application and audience for whom the assignment is intended.

Note: For the record, we are not necessarily convinced that grades are bad for a student's self-esteem or motivation. In fact, nowhere in the text do we recommend a wholesale dismissal of the grading process. However, we *do* believe that teachers tend to grade homework assignments for compliance rather than learning and that this practice sends the wrong message about the goals of meaningful homework.

FAMILY CHALLENGES

6. How will I address the challenges that stem from the varying levels of socioeconomic status among my students' families?

Students do not have equal access to the money needed to buy materials for projects, to computers with Internet access in their homes, or even to pencils and paper. Arrangements must be made to ensure that no students are barred from completing meaningful homework assignments because of low socioeconomic status.

When money is needed to buy materials, attempt to provide such materials for the student yourself. If this is not possible, seek outside sources to aid in the purchase of necessary materials (e.g., mini grants, community groups, and individual donors). Also, assist students in finding resources in their community, such as Internet access at the local library, use of the school library, and community centers. A traveling classroom backpack could even be filled with the basic necessities of paper, pencils, crayons, markers, glue, and more. Students could then sign up to use the backpack on particular days when they know it might be needed. In addition, asset-based assignments, as discussed in this text, use the talents, gifts, and strengths that exist within individual students and families regardless of socioeconomic status. Because it draws on things that already exist, asset-oriented homework minimizes the problems related to access to materials that often arise with traditional homework assignments. Socioeconomic status does not need to restrict the access students have to meaningful homework assignments as long as students are given whatever assistance they need.

7. What happens if there is no one at home willing or able to assist a student in completing homework assignments?

While this is a reality for some students, and one that requires sensitivity, it should not be used to justify a lack of meaningfulness in homework. Parents or other adult family members should remain the first option, and all it may take to gain their support is a simple conversation to convince them of the validity of the task. However, if parents or other adult family members are not an option, sit with the student and discuss other possibilities such as a member of the extended family, a coach, or a youth pastor.

Discussing alternatives may provide some insight into the student's situation at home and give you an opportunity to assist in the resource identification process. If the student's parents are not available, perhaps other adults would be willing to assist. As a last resort, draw on adults within the school like volunteers, PTA members, or supervisory and instructional support staff. Assignments that involve adults may require some additional planning in order to provide sufficient time and opportunity for the task to be completed. In cases where finding an adult proves problematic, teachers should exercise flexibility with regard to the assignment.

When involving adults in meaningful homework practices, communication and clarity of expectations should remain top priorities. It is vital that adults understand that the assignments are not meant to test content knowledge but rather to draw on their opinions and experiences related to the topic. Adult opinions and experiences that are shared with the class can add depth and perspective to classroom discussion. The end goal is a more robust and grounded understanding of the topic being studied.

Bear in mind that adults (particularly those with children) tend to be busy, so exercise restraint in regards to the number of questions or the time required to complete the tasks. This will go a long way towards garnering the necessary support.

8. What will I do about students who live in two households?

Establish a routine early in the year that guarantees a way for both families to get information about assignments. A class Web site, e-mail, phone calls, the postal service, or even something as simple as two copies of all communication, including homework assignments, are possible solutions. Another possibility is a daily planner with class information and a list of homework assignments that travels with students who move between households.

Which family will assist with each assignment? Depending on the structure of the assignment, including its length, a student might need to involve both households. It is usually best to consider this question ahead of time and prepare some options from which the student can choose. For example, if an assignment calls for a student to survey family members about a topic, you can privately ask the student to choose whether to pick one household or both to participate. Another possibility is to rotate the assignments between the two households so the student doesn't feel penalized by being asked to complete two assignments.

Long-term assignments can pose a problem if the student will move between the households during the course of the assignment. Plan to communicate with the second household after the assignment has begun and help the student to remain organized despite moving between the homes. Secondly, check in with the student more frequently to be sure that the assignment hasn't been derailed. For example, if the two households don't communicate regularly, each parent might think that the assignment is being worked on at the other household. Teacher communication with both households can prevent such misconceptions from occurring.

Finally, allow the student and family some freedom to adapt the assignments to match their individual situation. As long as the goals of the assignment are met, being flexible will encourage both families to be more supportive, and the student will be more likely to participate and be successful.

TEACHER CHALLENGES

9. Due to the constraints on my time, I can only allot limited minutes to designing meaningful home assignments. How can I get the most out of the time that I do have?

Think about meaningful assignments as falling along a continuum with basic skills practice at one end and authentic opportunities to apply knowledge and skills at the other. Consider ways to make incremental changes towards the more meaningful and authentic opportunities end of the spectrum. These changes need not take a lot of time. Start small, by simply tweaking existing assignments. Then reflect on how the changes you made produced an increase in student enthusiasm and overall motivation. Then repeat the process. Remember, it may be helpful to adopt the long view: these types of assignments may ultimately save time.

Another useful strategy is to work with colleagues in your district or building to share the creative workload. Perhaps teachers could be given release time to work on changing a set of their upcoming assignments. Take advantage of the time that does exist (e.g., lunchroom conversations, grade-level or departmental meetings, etc.) and share your results.

Other strategies to consider include focusing on assignments that accentuate one particular inquiry skill (such as asking questions, collecting and analyzing data, or summarizing findings and reflecting) or one principle of meaningful homework (such as extending education to the home and community by involving adults in responsible ways, providing for expanded meaningfulness and life application of school learning, or personalizing the curriculum and reflecting on the here and now). Teachers could also direct their efforts into one specific subject area or class. Our point is that these changes need not be overwhelming in size and scope. Start small but dream big!

10. I just cannot think of ideas for these meaningful homework assignments. What can I do to get the ideas flowing?

Almost everybody faces this issue from time to time. One way to get started is to revisit your goals to make sure they are appropriate. Then brainstorm goal-related activities that apply to real life.

A second possibility is to ask students how they believe a particular instructional goal might apply to real life. You will be surprised at the possibilities students come up with! Instead of debating which idea is best, give students choices and be prepared for some engaging in-class conversations. Students appreciate having a voice, and when they are motivated because their ideas are used, they will do amazing things!

To generate more ideas, use all that this book has to offer. If you have read only the chapter (from Chapters 7 to 10) that pertains to your particular grade level, we encourage you to read the remaining chapters. Many of the assignments described there can be modified to meet your needs at your specific grade.

11. In my district, parents have online access to their child's grades, and some parents expect new grades to be entered every day. This type of homework does not lend itself to being graded every day, if it is even graded at all. How do I interact with parents who desire this continual grade updating?

It cannot be stressed enough that clear communication with parents must be established. A letter sent home at the beginning of the year explaining grading policies (including the frequency with which parents can expect to see new grades added online) is critical in establishing a foundation of communication. Also, schedule an open house so parents can ask questions about grading practices. Teachers must be clear in their goals and their structuring of meaningful homework assignments, and they must be able to articulate these ideas to parents and school administrators. The commitment to meaningful homework is also a commitment to educating parents about the rationale behind such assignments. A change in the "culture of homework" is the goal, helping parents to understand that a daily grade that can be seen online may not have as much impact on student learning as a sustained, worthwhile assignment that firmly cements the topics discussed in class and their relationship to the real world. In addition, teachers must not give up the benefits of actual conversation with parents. True understanding of a student's progress does not transfer well electronically. Generally, it is best attained through thoughtful, person-to-person interactions.

To aid in the transition to meaningful homework, teachers can continue using some sort of grading system while working to change the perceptions and attitudes of schools and families. One option is to simply record whether students have "met expectations" or "not met expectations." This could be recorded online, giving parents a checkpoint to see if their child is completing and meeting the expectations of each homework assignment.

ADMINISTRATOR CHALLENGES

12. As an administrator, how can I support teachers as they strive to "push the envelope" in their use of meaningful homework as a learning tool?

A supportive administrator can provide teachers with the resources and time to begin researching and talking together about homework. It is important and valuable for staff to spend time learning about and discussing the areas where they plan to focus their attention. For resources, the administrator can provide interested staff members with books or conference time that they can use to begin developing a deeper understanding of successful homework strategies.

During this process, the building administrator can be a role model for teachers by participating in a book study group or research team. The group, formed of a representative sampling of the staff, can help to make decisions and encourage staff to begin making decisions about homework policies and practices.

District policies can range from vague to confusing to restrictive. The administrator can help to clarify those policies and, if necessary, give permission to suspend old expectations as the staff begins to craft new ones.

The principal can also be a communication bridge between district-level administrators and teaching staff in the building. Understanding teachers' goals and communicating them to upper-level administration can pave the way for teachers to push the envelope and try new strategies related to homework.

The administrator might also be called upon to help communicate with parents who are confused or concerned by changes to a familiar homework policy. Teachers will be much more comfortable and likely to make significant changes knowing that their administrator will support and assist them.

13. What kind of staff development can be used to help teachers grow in the understanding and use of meaningful homework?

The most effective staff development involves faculty buy-in to the proposed idea. Ideally it includes an element of teacher choice in the topic, the information-gathering process, the working subgroups, or the delivery of content. Some teachers like to review literature first, others like to start by having an invited speaker stimulate their thinking, and still others like to observe in classrooms where the specific initiative is being enacted. Teachers should also be involved in setting the agenda for each professional development session.

Allocating time for staff development is essential. It could be a replacement for faculty meetings or an alternative to all-district faculty development sessions. Having members of the leadership team participate in the sessions will have an enormous payoff.

SCHOOL CULTURE CHALLENGES

14. Our school policy clearly specifies the nature of expected homework assignments. The principles outlined in this book are quite different from what my district mandates. How can I work within this system?

It is possible to satisfy district mandates and implement meaningful homework at the same time. First, find out whether the supposed school policy is truly mandated. If the school policy does differ from the principles outlined in this book, then possibilities for meaningful homework can be explored on a "pilot" basis, beginning with one subject or one class. Teachers can share plans for the meaningful homework pilot program with a curriculum leader and communicate that the purpose of the initiative is to enhance the current curriculum rather than replace it. Teachers have the power to change school culture, starting with what they can control in their own classrooms. When the results of meaningful homework are collected and shared with others, the changes in how homework is utilized will speak for themselves.

If teachers anticipate resistance, they should be strategic about when and how they involve other people in the implementation of meaningful homework. Although it is ideal to involve administration when implementing new initiatives, sometimes it is beneficial to start small and test new ideas that will elicit the support of parents and students. "Working with the willing" can help teachers build momentum for positive change.

Some of the most important initiatives that positively impact student learning occur on the fringes of school culture. It is the professional responsibility of teachers to create, analyze, and reflect on contexts for learning that can make the time spent in and out of school more productive for students.

15. I find that there is pressure from other teachers in my school to assign traditional homework assignments. What will happen to my students next year when their homework will look much different than what we complete in my classroom?

If gifted professionals knew for sure that their students would face boring or ineffective teachers next year, would they shift their plans and replicate bad practice? Of course not! Remember also that most teachers will probably continue to assign some traditional homework.

Over the course of the year, teachers can consider sharing with their colleagues what they and their students are experiencing with more authentic home assignments. The students and some parents will vocalize the differences, hopefully leading other teachers to embrace new possibilities.

CONCLUSION

Change is gradual. It cannot be mandated. It starts with the individual and slowly seeps into the system. However, making practice more public is a powerful way to influence others.

Challenges can be growth producing if viewed as problems to be solved. The authors of this text are counting on you to push the envelope and afford students learning possibilities heretofore not imagined.

THAT'S ME . . . NOW!

Early in the textbook, the authors shared some of their former frustrations about homework and asked you to identify which ones you were currently facing.

Now you have read the text and hopefully have begun making some changes in your practice.

Here we ask you to check in again to see where you are in your thinking and to identify the shifts that you've made.

I am no longer inundated with homework papers to check. Now when I'm chilling on the sofa after dinner, I'm mulling over all the new home assignments I can design.

While the pressure from NCLB, state standards, and content coverage haven't eased a bit, I find myself worrying less. Students are actually doing more content prep at home, and I'm convinced it is because the in-class conversations are so much more authentic. Students actually see the connections to their lives.

I'm thrilled with the turn-in rate of home activities. Using authentic data as an integral part of instruction is without a doubt the key.

I'm beginning to figure out that no matter what the district mandates, the pacing guide is just a guide. My students meet all the requirements—and so much more. They have so much capacity!

I'm still getting e-mails. A few parents complain because the assignments often call for them to talk with their kids, but most of the messages involve apologies because they didn't complete the assignment on time or requests for extensions.

Dogs don't seem to like the revised approach to homework. The excuses have turned into apologies such as "My dad was out of town, and I need to the weekend to complete the interview," or "Grandma had bridge, and I didn't get a chance to talk to her yet."

The principal remains a stickler about time allocations for homework, but it is no longer an issue. I can't believe how much extra time students spend on the assignments.

I continue to sandwich in the necessary skill-building practice exercises with the authentic home assignments.

I'm excited that the students talk to one another about their homework. They learn so much from each other.

Since I have begun building in mini skill lessons, the homework assignment completion rate is dramatically higher, and the quality continues to dazzle me.

We have amazing class discussions, and if I forget to give the nightly home assignment, students invariably will remind me.

I am continuing to gain confidence in developing home assignments that are authentic, meaningful, and far more robust than the district's packaged curriculum.

Parent complaints about kids failing have all but vanished. Families of special-needs students are generally ecstatic because of the positive changes they have seen in their children now that they can contribute to class discussions.

Enhanced family involvement in homework has increased dramatically. I couldn't be happier.

Appendix A

*Completed Homework
Design Planning Form*

Completed Homework Design Planning Form

Humanizing the Auto Industry

Principles of Meaningful Homework		Inquiry Skills
Check those that are incorporated.		*Check those that will be utilized.*
☒ Providing for expanded meaningfulness and life application of school learning		☒ Ask questions.
☐ Constructing meaning in natural ways and expanding a sense of self-efficacy		☒ Identify problems.
☐ Extending education to the home and community by engaging adults in interesting and responsible ways		☒ Collect and analyze data.
		☐ Make observations.
☐ Taking advantage of the students' diversity by using it as a learning resource		☐ Choose sources and collect evidence.
☐ Personalizing the curriculum and reflecting on the here and now		☒ Summarize findings and reflect.
		☐ _____
☐ Exploiting learning opportunities that are not cost-effective on school time		☐ _____
☒ Keeping the curriculum up-to-date		☐ _____

Relevant Standards (national, state and/or district)

National Standard: Individuals, groups, and institutions

Michigan Standard: Explain how changes in the U.S. economy impact levels of employment and unemployment.

Assignment Goals

✓ Students will understand how labor unions have impacted workers' lives and our economy throughout history while continuing to be important today.

✓ Students will understand that changes can be achieved if citizens assert their collective power and question how that power is used.

✓ Students will consider the role of unions in the auto industry through multiple perspectives.

Assignment Description

Students collaborate with a family member first to discover the ways that they are connected to the auto industry. They begin by determining which family members or friends work in the industry. They then speculate together about what would happen if the auto industry left Michigan, examining additional businesses, organizations, or institutions that would be impacted by the departure (e.g., state tax revenue). This information is shared with the class, and students' connections with the auto industry are charted on poster paper.

Students then participate in another assignment that helps them understand advanced content related to the range of benefits that workers receive. Students survey adults in their family along with neighbors to tabulate their thoughts related to health insurance, salary, and work conditions. This assignment creates the foundation for understanding workers' needs and rights and allows students to access advanced concepts related to these issues.

Finally, students discuss with their family what they have learned about the history of unions in their state. They share their new understanding of the historical significance and origin of unions and discuss with a family member how economic issues related to unions connect to universal ideas like fairness, representation, and the common good. Students investigate whether or not their parents belong to a union and the advantages (benefits) and disadvantages (costs) of union membership. They are prompted to discuss these issues from multiple perspectives.

Assignment Timeline

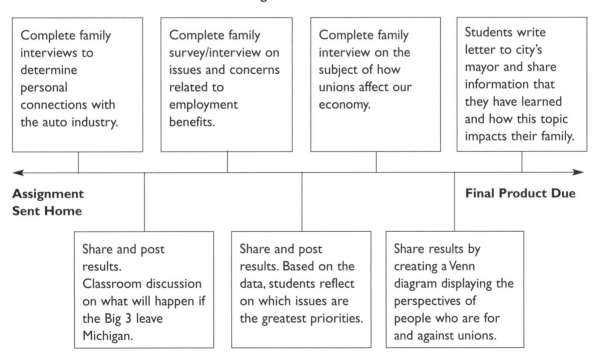

Student Assets	Family Assets	Community Assets
• Unrelenting interest in "fairness" • Curious about cost-benefit analysis • Classroom experience • Organic Goodie Simulation (Bigelow, 1994)	• Family members and neighbors that work for the auto industry. • Concerns about employment, health insurance, retirement, regardless of job.	Field trip to auto plant Guest speakers: • Retired auto executive • UAW union leader • Nonunion auto worker

Student Input and Voice

Students watch CNN video of city's mayor describing issues related to unions and the auto industry. After the video clip, students generate a list of questions that they have about unions. Students then work to group their questions into two major categories of issues that they want to learn more about. Possible categories could include the history of unions in our state, advantages and disadvantages of union membership, workers' point of view versus that of executives, impact on competition, union vocabulary, etc. Students' questions will be integrated into family surveys and interviews.

Communication With Families	Necessary Organizational Tools and Resources
Check those that will be used. ☒ Letter to go home ☐ Open house planned ☒ E-mail to be sent ☐ Phone calls ☐ Home visits ☐ Classroom Web page to be used ☒ Inclusion in classroom newsletter ☒ Student planner ☐ _____ ☐ _____ ☐ _____	Data collection forms for use in the interview assignments are listed above. Some sample titles for creating forms are as follows: • Finding Personal Connections With the Auto Industry • Issues and Concerns Related to Employment Benefits • Unions and Our Economy Sample forms follow below. Student results from the forms will be tallied, charted, or graphed. Resources: • *History for Kids: Labor Yesterday and Today* • Nonfiction background information packet about unions adapted from www.news.bbc.co.uk

Instructional Uses of Assignment

Results from the assignment are shared in various ways. Students share their results with partners, in small groups, and in whole-class discussions. At the end of the unit, students participate in a mock talk show that requires them to take on the role of either an auto executive, a union steward, a worker who is a union member, a worker who is not a union member, a psychologist, or a great-grandmother who was a child laborer. During the talk show, they discuss and defend their thinking by using examples from their homework. Students then reflect on their learning by writing a letter to the mayor to share the information that they have gathered on the topic along with recommendations.

Possible Extensions	**Integration**
• Students determine ways to increase student representation in decision-making processes in school or the classroom. • Students examine how "power" has been used or misused throughout history and in modern organizations.	• Read aloud *Lyddie* by Katherine Paterson. • Use in op-ed writing unit. • Write letter to mayor. • Examine tables, graphs, and maps for data related to unions in our country. • Use in nonfiction reading strategies. ☐ Collaboration with another teacher(s) required.

Anticipated Barriers

• Families may perceive this as a debate in which they voice their opinion about unions. This can be an emotional topic. Emotion is good because it shows that it is important. I will make clear in the initial family letter that our purpose is not to debate whether unions are good or bad for our economy. Instead, our goal is to understand that there can be multiple perspectives on issues and that this topic has a direct impact on the people in our state. We're focused on learning about how power is used or misused in the workplace.

• Parents might not know about this topic. I will provide them with a packet with current information.

• Families might think that their profession and income are important for this assignment. I will reassure them in the initial family letter that specific details related to their income are not important or requested. I will explain this by sharing with families the big ideas for the unit and ask that they focus on these ideas during their discussions.

State Economics Unit: Home Learning Assignment
"Finding Personal Connection With the Auto Industry"
What if the Big 3 leave Michigan?

Dear Families,

We are continuing to study economics, and we are now narrowing our focus to uncover new understandings related to the automobile industry here in Michigan and around the world. On Friday, we will be joined by another General Motors employee to kick off this section of our study. He will discuss the many different jobs that people do working for GM. We will be using the auto industry to apply basic economic concepts. We will also be focusing on the concept of "power" in the workplace along with issues related to the history of labor in America. These are important concepts, so I hope that you are as excited as I am to jump into this amazing and currently meaningful topic!

DUE FRIDAY—Be ready to share with our guest speaker!
Note: We will try to finish math study links in class to free you up to answer these with a family member.

Discuss and answer with a family member. (There is a FRONT and BACK.)

With a family member, think about all of the ways that your family is or has been connected to the auto industry. Consider friends and neighbors. Connections can include working directly for the industry, but think about other connections as well. What stories about the auto industry can you share? Be specific, meaning don't just mention that "Uncle Harry worked for Ford". What did he actually do for Ford?

_____

_____

_____

List ways that you think the auto industry impacts our families, our town, and the world today. Also list the impacts it has had in the past. What role does it play in our state, and why is this important to your life now? Basically, in your own words, why should we care to study this?

_____

_____

_____

List 2–3 other *issues* related to the auto industry that you think we should study:

_____

_____

_____

List at least 3 *researchable questions* or concerns that you and your family member have about the auto industry. Do you have any questions to ask a GM worker?

_____

_____

_____

State Economics Unit: Home Learning Assignment
"Issues and Concerns Related to Employment Benefits"

Dear Families,

We have been studying economics during the last few weeks. Your child has learned to apply basic economic concepts, such as scarcity, opportunity cost, supply and demand, etc. to his or her own life. Students have been focusing on Michigan's economy, specifically the auto industry.

As you know, the economy is an extremely important topic these days. The question is, can we make this topic interesting and powerful for students? We are now starting to study the historical and contemporary issue of "power" in the workplace. This topic has the potential to be very interesting and important.

To get us started, we need your help in grasping the concerns that people have about their employment. We need to form a basic understanding of health insurance, wages, benefits, and work conditions. These can be complicated ideas, but it is amazing to see what students can understand! In class, students have been generating a long list of questions related to employment.

Please know that your profession and income are *not* important for this assignment. Your personal experiences and real ideas/concerns about being employed *are* important, and I'm hoping that we can gather diverse information.

Please know that there are no right or wrong answers to the questions that your child will ask you. Please help your child as much as you can and feel free to expand on the questions or encourage your child to consider additional issues.

On Thursday, students will participate in a simulation called "The Organic Goodie Simulation." This lesson will let students experience some of the pressures that lead workers to organize. Set in an imaginary society, it challenges students to think about questions like these: Can people work together to accomplish needed changes? If so, what circumstances encourage this unity? This simulation is a lot of fun and will hopefully help students understand some of the reasons why workers have developed unions and other organizations over the course of history.

With our social studies focus on Michigan, we will examine the hot-button topic of unions. We understand that this topic can stir some emotions with adults, but our goal is *not* to debate whether unions are good or bad for our economy. Instead, it is to understand that there can be multiple perspectives on issues and that this topic has a direct impact on the people in our state's economy. The big idea is that sometimes power can be misused and create unproductive or unfair conditions in the workplace.

We will end our unit with a mock televison show styled after *Oprah Winfrey,* demonstrating what we have learned. Each student will take on the role of one of the following:

- Auto executive
- Union steward
- Psychologist (who studies power)
- Investor
- Auto worker who is unionized
- Auto worker who is nonunionized
- Great-grandmother who was a child laborer

I am in the process of locating real people who represent these roles for students to interview. If you know of anyone, please let me know. During the next few weeks, we will need your assistance in preparing for our show. Thank you for all your support and for having such unique and gifted children! Please do not hesitate to call if you have any questions.

Sincerely,
Rob

State Economics Unit: Home Learning Assignment
"Issues and Concerns Related to Employment Benefits"
Health Insurance Family Interview

1. Please explain to me the basics of how your (our) health care plan works.

   _____

   _____

   _____

2. Have you had the same health insurance throughout your life? ____Yes ____No
   If not, how has it changed (e.g., deductible, coverage, etc.)?

   _____

   _____

   _____

3. What do you like about your health insurance, and what do you wish was different about it?

   _____

   _____

   _____

4. What role does your employer play in deciding what health insurance you have? Do you have
   options? If so, tell me about the options and why you have the one you do.

   _____

   _____

   _____

5. Will you have health care after you retire? Please explain.

   _____

   _____

   _____

6. At what age will I not be covered under your health care plan?

   _____

   _____

   _____

7. When I turn _____ years old, I will need to get my own health care.
   What other questions or concerns do I have about health insurance? List at least two.

   _____

   _____

   _____

Wages and Benefits Family Interview

On Commission	Hourly	Salary (same amount of money every month)

1. Which of the three kinds of wages listed above do you receive? _____

2. What is taken out of your wages, and who takes it (i.e., state, federal government, etc.)? Please give me details.

   _____

   _____

   _____

3. Do you have a contract? If so, what does your contract guarantee? Can your employer change your contract whenever they want? How is your contract determined?

   _____

   _____

   _____

4. Who decides how much money you make?

   _____

   _____

   _____

5. Do you get paid differently based on performance, attendance, etc.? Describe what incentives you receive for "doing a good job" or an above-standard job.

   _____

   _____

   _____

6. Do you get paid sick days? How many? Who is involved in determining how many sick days you receive?

   _____

   _____

   _____

7. Can you show me one of your pay stubs? I notice . . .

   _____

   _____

   _____

8. What other questions or concerns do I have about wages and benefits? List at least two.

   _____

   _____

   _____

Work Conditions and Safety Family Interview

1. What do you like about your work conditions?

_____

_____

_____

2. What do you not like about your work conditions?

_____

_____

_____

3. Describe your physical work environment (e.g., temperature, lighting, cleanliness of facility, furniture, etc.)

_____

_____

_____

4. Who determines how many hours and what type of work you do?

_____

_____

_____

5. What do you do if you are given too much work? Do you ever feel overwhelmed or overworked?

_____

_____

_____

6. Have you ever been treated unfairly in the workplace? Please describe.

_____

_____

_____

7. Please describe at least one conflict situation or disagreement that you have had in the workplace. Can you describe a time when you have disagreed with your boss? Can you describe a time when you have disagreed with a coworker or someone who works for you?

_____

_____

_____

8. If you or your coworkers have concerns or complaints about your work conditions, what do you do to get those concerns resolved?

_____

_____

_____

9. What benefits do you receive?

_____

_____

_____

10. Do you get breaks and, if so, what kinds (e.g., lunch breaks? bathroom breaks?)? Who decides when you take these breaks?

_____

_____

_____

11. Do you have to travel for your work? Who pays for your travel?

_____

_____

_____

12. Is safety ever an issue for the work that you do?

_____

_____

_____

13. What perks do you receive (e.g., company car, laptop, cell phone)?

_____

_____

_____

14. Do you have to pay for anything to do your job (for example, gas for a vehicle)?

_____

_____

_____

15. What other questions or concerns do you have about work conditions and safety? List at least two.

_____

_____

_____

State Economics Unit: Home Learning Assignment
"Unions and Our Economy"

The student should ask a family member or community member the questions below when filling out this form. List the name of the person interviewed here:

_____

Note to Interviewee: Each student has a copy of the magazine *History for Kids: Labor Yesterday and Today*. This may be helpful to you if you are unfamiliar with the topic or if you would like more information.

Questions for Interviewee:

1. What is a union? What do you know about unions?

_____
_____
_____

2. What role have unions played in our state's history?
   Why do you think they were created? Have they changed? How?

_____
_____
_____

3. Why do you think some organizations/businesses have them and others do not?

_____
_____
_____

4. Do you belong to a union? _____ Yes ___No
   If not, would you want to belong to a union? Why or why not?

_____
_____
_____

   If you do belong to a union, do you feel that you benefit from being in a union? How? Did you get to choose to be in the union?

_____
_____
_____

5. In what other ways are you connected to unions? Do you have relatives that belong to unions? Do you have any family stories related to unions?

_____
_____
_____

6. Unions—Positive and Negative Impacts on our Economy

Why would anyone be critical of unions?

What role do unions play in our current economic situation?

Why would anyone be opposed to having unions?

Union Positives +	Union Negatives −

Two questions that *we* have about this topic:

1. _____

2. _____

REFERENCES

Bigelow, B. (1994). *Rethinking our classrooms: Teaching for equity and justice.* Milwaukee, WI: Rethinking Schools.

Appendix B

Early Elementary Data Collection Tools

A data collection tool is aligned with each of the grade-level examples. They are labeled within each example and presented in the order they appear in the text.

DATA COLLECTION TOOLS

B.1: *My Ancestors,* Early Elementary Social Studies

B.2: *Weather Reporting You Can Believe,* Early Elementary Science

B.3: *The Clothing Museum,* Early Elementary Social Studies

B.4: *Pairs Are Everywhere,* Early Elementary Math

B.5: *Traveling Mascot,* Early Elementary Language Arts

Appendix B.I

My Ancestors Early Elementary Social Studies

Social Studies Homework   <u>DUE BY WEDNESDAY</u>!

Name _____

Almost everyone who lives in America has ancestors that came from another country. Do you know the country or countries that your ancestors came from?

_____

_____

Do you have any special traditions or foods that go along with where your ancestors came from?

_____

_____

Does your family have any special celebrations or special ways to celebrate that are traditions in your family? (For example, birthdays or holidays)

_____

_____

Appendix   B.2

Weather Reporting You Can Believe
Early Elementary Science

WEATHER WORDS

Name _____

We have just begun a new unit about weather. During our unit, we will be discussing places to find out weather information and which sources are best. Your child's job is to find places to gather weather information and list them here. Then please help your child create a list of possible weather words that describe temperature, precipitation, wind, etc. We will be using these words in class as we keep a weather journal describing the weather outside. Please make sure your child finds at least five weather sources and lists them below along with weather words learned from each source. Then make sure your child brings the list to school so our class can create a list of weather words together!

Source	Weather Words
1.	
2.	
3.	
4.	
5.	

Appendix B.3

The Clothing Museum
Early Elementary Social Studies

THE CLOTHING TREASURE HUNT

Name _____

Your job will be to go through closets and dressers in your house to find the 25 things listed below. When you find something, write a quick description of it on the line next to the type of clothing that it is. So for example, if you find a T-shirt that is 100 percent cotton, write "T-shirt" on the line next to "Clothing that is 100 percent cotton."

Try to use each piece of clothing only once.

Return this list to class along with your favorite clothing item so we can put it in our class museum!

Example: Clothing that is blue _____*jeans*_____

List of 25 Things to Find:

1. Clothing that is 100 percent cotton _____

2. Clothing that is part wool _____

3. Clothing with a cotton blend _____

4. Clothing with silk _____

5. Clothing with fur (real or fake) _____

6. Clothing with nylon _____

7. Clothing for protection _____

8. Clothing for communication _____

9. Clothing for modesty _____

10. Clothing for recreation _____

11. Clothing for decoration _____

12. Clothing with hooks _____

13. Clothing with Velcro _____

14. Clothing with more than five buttons _____

15. Clothing with one button _____

16. Clothing made by hand _____

17. Clothing at least 20 years old _____

18. Clothing bought at a store _____

19. Clothing bought at a garage sale _____

20. Clothing that was "handed-down" _____

21. Clothing that was a gift _____

22. Clothing to keep you warm _____

23. Clothing to keep you cool _____

24. Clothing to keep you dry _____

25. Clothing for fun _____

Score Yourself

0–10	You're just getting started!
11–15	Now you are looking good!
16–20	What a super searcher!
21–25	Certified Clothing Detective!

Appendix B.4

Pairs Are Everywhere
Early Elementary Math

MATH HOMEWORK   NAME _____

COUNTING BY 2S   DUE JANUARY 15

We have been working on counting by 2s. We noticed that many things come in groups of two, like eyes, shoes, and bicycle tires. Look around and find something else that comes in groups of two. Draw several of them in the box below and then count them by 2s.

"There were _____ _____,"
said _____.

Appendix B.5

Traveling Mascot
Early Elementary Language Arts

Dear Families:

The newest member of our class is Amelia the Cow. We named her Amelia after the aviator because she loves to have adventures. Amelia will get a chance to come home for at least one weekend with each child.

Amelia has her own backpack and a special journal to record her adventures and the fun that she has. When your child brings home the journal, please help your child to record the events for each day on a page. This is exactly the same writing we do in class; we call it a "small moments story." These small moments stories have a beginning, middle, and end. They include specific, true details that help the reader visualize what happened. Feel free to use pictures or photographs to help plan the story.

You and your child might also decide to include some artifacts from the visit. Those things can be added to Amelia's backpack. Be sure to keep track of all her belongings and return them to school together. In the front pocket, you will also find pencils, crayons, and a glue stick to use.

Look over your schedule for this year and request a time to have Amelia join your family for exciting adventures or just a quiet weekend. We are looking forward to reading all of your great stories!

✶ ✶

Student name _____

Our family would like Amelia to visit on _____.

Please return this to school by next Friday!

Appendix C

Upper Elementary Data Collection Tools

A data collection tool is aligned with each of the grade-level examples. They are labeled within each example and presented in the order they appear in the text.

DATA COLLECTION TOOLS

C.1: *Extending Democracy via Voter Registration*, Upper Elementary Social Studies

C.2: *Putting Wheelchair Accessibility Rights Into Motion*, Upper Elementary Science

C.3: *Locating Problems for Editorials*, Upper Elementary English Language Arts

C.4: *Beyond Metric Conversion*, Upper Elementary Mathematics

C.5: *Artistic Visionaries for a Better Future*, Upper Elementary Art

---

Appendix C.1

Extending Democracy via Voter Registration
Upper Elementary Social Studies

Name of Person to Whom I Talked	Are They Registered to Vote? Yes or No	We Talked About . . .	After Talking With This Person, I Now Wonder. I Want to Learn More About . . .

CAMPAIGN 2008 CONVERSATION STARTERS

Social Studies Standard: Explain important rights and how, when, and where American citizens demonstrate their responsibilities by participating in government. Explain responsibilities of citizenship (initiating changes in laws or policy, respecting the law, being informed and attentive to public issues, paying taxes, registering to vote, and voting knowledgeably).

Use these questions when talking to your parents, grandparents, brothers, sisters, friends, or anyone else (except for strangers) about the issues and ideas of the 2008 election. Note: With simple modifications, these questions could be used at any level over time.

1. What do you know about the 2008 presidential candidates?

2. What would you still like to know about them?

3. What are the main qualities that you look for in a leader? Why?

4. In your opinion, what are the most important issues facing the next president?

5. Do you think the new president will face more challenges than the last? Why or why not?

6. How important do you think a candidate's age, race, or gender should be in weighing his or her overall ability to lead?

7. If you could give "presidential report cards" to any presidents in U.S. history, to whom would you give the highest grades and to whom would you give the lowest? Why?

8. Who do you predict will be elected? What evidence leads you to this prediction?

9. How much do you think voters have the right to know about a presidential candidate's personal life?

10. What issues do you think should receive more media coverage, and why?

11. What makes 2008 an historic election year, and why?

12. Who should be able to vote? Who shouldn't? Why?

13. How would you convince a friend, family or community member to vote?

Our Government and Civics "Wonders" So Far . . .

- How have peoples' complaints helped change this area?
- Where did the idea to make 3 branches come from?
- How were constitutional rights determined?
- Why can only adults vote?
- Why can't kids vote?
- Has kid voting ever been considered possible?
- Why did the United States choose to be a democracy?
- Why couldn't African Americans, women, and Native Americans vote?
- How will Obama and McCain improve the economy?
- What are Obama's and McCain's policies for lowering college tuition?
- Why didn't McCain run in 2004?
- What ideas do Obama and McCain have for helping the less fortunate (e.g., homeless people, hungry people, hurricane victims)?

- How long has voting been going on?
- If kids could have the right to vote, what would it look like?
- Has a group of kids ever stood up and made a change in government?
- How did women convince others that they deserved the right to vote?
- What are McCain's and Obama's education policies?
- When was the first time anyone voted?
- What are McCain's and Obama's environmental policies?
- Can candidates vote?
- How did the candidates get to be candidates?
- Will gas prices affect college tuition?
- Why does Obama want to raise the minimum wage and McCain want to keep it the same?
- Do homeless people vote?
- Is it possible to stop global warming within ten years?
- What if all of the homeless people voted?
- How can we allow Internet voting so more people could vote?
- How can I improve the quality of public schools?
- Is it possible to make the laws better?
- What if only kids made laws?
- How can kids have a bigger impact on the election?
- How can I improve the government and laws?
- Is it possible for kids to write a law?
- What if there were no laws?
- How can we help government?
- If I had money, how could I help the government?
- Is it possible to have a tie in the election?
- What if both the president and the vice president die?
- How can we help improve the economy?
- If I had a house and lost my job, how could I pay my taxes?
- If I had fifty people, how could I get them all to volunteer in the community?
- Is it possible to vote on more than one day?
- How can we get more people to vote?
- If I had good ideas, how could I help the campaign?
- Is it possible to get all the grownups in Michigan to vote?
- Is it possible to live and work in the USA and not be able to vote?
- What if everybody who could, voted?
- If I had money, how could I help build or maintain roads, businesses, buildings, and other stuff?
- What if a senator breaks a law?
- How can we help the environment?
- How can I improve college tuition?
- How can we get people involved and interested in government every year?
- What would happen to the school if we did not have government?
- What are different reasons people protest in the United States?
- What has been the most important protest in reforming laws?
- What if protesting were not allowed?
- Is it possible for all of the government leaders to meet in the same place?
- When comparing the United States (representing democracy) with North Korea (representing dictatorship), which country's citizens are happier?
- When comparing Michigan's economy with Ohio's, which has more money?

- What caused the Iraq war?
- Is it possible to perform any of the government's services on your own (e.g., road work)?
- Is it possible to be a governor and a president at the same time?
- What if a candidate for president dies the week of the election?
- How can we help our preferred candidate win?
- If I had a million dollars to spend on the election, how could I use it the most effectively to help a candidate win?
- How can I improve voter participation?
- What if taxes are too high?
- When comparing the U.S. with Britain, in which country do citizens pay more taxes?
- What would happen if we didn't have taxes?
- How can we lower taxes?
- How can I improve the public services provided to people in Haslett?
- What if we ran out of money to pay for taxes?
- Why did the Taliban attack us during 9/11?
- Have citizens ever protested taxes?
- What does "civic virtue" mean?
- When did our government discover that they needed taxes?
- Does the president have to pay taxes?
- How can kids help contribute time and money to help solve problems in the community?
- How can I improve our environment?
- What if no one volunteered in the community?
- When comparing Haslett to Williamston, which town has more citizen volunteers?
- How does volunteering affect the economy?

Appendix C.2

Putting Wheelchair Accessibility Rights Into Motion
Upper Elementary Science

Simple Machine Observation

Directions:

Explore how simple machines are used in your life by sketching images of the machines listed below that are being used to make everyday work in our community easier. Record examples that you feel are important to others' lives.

Lever	Wheel & Axle	Inclined Plane
Pulley	Screw	Wedge

Reflection:

What would life be like if you did not have simple machines? Considering your examples above, what challenges would you face?

_____

_____

_____

_____

Appendix C.3

Locating Problems for Editorials
Upper Elementary Language Arts

Name: _____

Locating Problems for Editorials

Problems Are Everywhere!

Big Idea

Successful editorial writers get ideas by collecting *problems* related to *issues* that they feel are important. Editorial writers often read, hear, or see something and then say, "That's not fair!" or, "I need to do something about that!" Editorial writers then use writing as a way to communicate their opinions on the topic to persuade other people, encourage thinking, and sometimes cause people to take action on the issue.

Directions:

We are collecting ideas for our editorials. Look in the newspaper, listen to the radio, watch the news, or talk with a family member to locate a problem that you could use in your editorial. If you choose to write about this problem, remember that it needs to be important to *you* and the *world*.

A Possible Editorial Topic/Theme Based on the Problem:

Summary of Problem or Issue Found List your ideas below. You will share these with your group tomorrow. If you find a newspaper article, please attach it to this page.	Source: newspaper, news, TV, magazines, movies, interviews
_____ _____ _____ _____ _____ _____ _____ _____	

Appendix C.4

Beyond Metric Conversion
Upper Elementary Mathematics

The Metric System: Family Member Life Experience Survey

Survey Issue:

Should the citizens of the United States increase efforts to transition to the modern metric system?

Directions:

Ask one or more family members the following class-generated questions. Record their responses to help prepare for our class discussion.

Person Surveyed: _____

Questions:

1. Tell me everything that you know about the metric system.

2. Do you think our country should *fully* adopt the metric system? _____ Yes _____ No

Why? _____

Advantages of Metric Conversion	Disadvantages of Metric Conversion

Life Activity	Metrics System Used?	
	Yes How?	No
School		
Travel outside of the United States		
Job		
Communication with friends or family outside of the United States		

Appendix C.5

Artistic Visionaries for a Better Future
Upper Elementary Art

My Social Issue: _____

Directions:

Investigate symbols, images, and ideas related to your social issue. Photograph, sketch, or use images from magazines and newspapers to create visual representations of your concern or issue. Express your concern for this issue within our community. Finally, discuss with a family member how your image represents your questions or concerns about this issue. When discussing your art, use the list of adjectives below or your own words to describe the piece that you have created.

Use the space below to list your ideas.

Possible Symbols	Possible Images or Scenes	Possible Adjectives

Adjective List:

Peaceful	Helpless	Energetic	Flowing
Symmetrical	Defiant	Lonely	Troubled
Asymmetrical	Hurt	Balanced	Frenetic
Fun	Lazy	Meticulous	Elegant
Playful	Thoughtless	Imaginative	Bold
Mysterious	Tired	Resourceful	Provocative
Frantic	Tender	Seamless	Soothing

Appendix D

Middle School Data Collection Tools

data collection tool is aligned with each of the grade-level examples. They are labeled within each example and presented in the order they appear in the text.

DATA COLLECTION TOOLS

D.1: *The Patterns Around Us*, Middle School Mathematics

D.2: *Reducing Your Carbon Footprint*, Middle School Science

D.3: *Building a Case for the Fine Arts*, Middle School Social Studies

D.4: *War Through the Generations*, Middle School English Language Arts

D.5: *The Media's Impact on Physical Health*, Middle School Physical Education

Appendix D.1

The Patterns Around Us
Middle School Mathematics

Directions: Complete the following table by recording where your picture was taken, describing what is in the picture, and describing the pattern you find in the picture.

Picture	Location	Picture Description	Description of Pattern
1			
2			
3			
4			

Appendix D.2

Reducing Your Carbon Footprint
Middle School Science

Directions: With the help of someone at home, answer the following questions. These data will then be used back at school to calculate your family's carbon footprint.

THE BASICS

1. How many people live in your home? _____

2. What is your household's primary heating source? _____

VEHICLES

How many vehicles does your household have? _____

	Vehicle 1	Vehicle 2	Vehicle 3	Vehicle 4
Average number of miles driven per week				
Average gas mileage (miles per gallon)				

HOME ENERGY

How much does your household use of the following each week:

Natural Gas (in dollars, thousand cubic feet, or therms)	
Electricity (in dollars or kilowatt-hours)	
Fuel Oil (in dollars or gallons)	
Propane (in dollars or gallons)	

WASTE

What do you recycle in your home?

	Yes	No
Aluminum and Steel Cans		
Plastic		
Glass		
Newspaper		
Magazines		

Appendix D.3

Building a Case for the Fine Arts
Middle School Social Studies

Directions: Select two people and record their names at the top of this table. Then interview each person, using the two provided questions as well as additional questions we will create in class. Record each answer and be prepared to discuss your results back in our classroom.

	Name:	**Name:**
What is your reaction to the proposal to suspend the Grades 5–12 fine arts program?		
What do you view as alternatives to suspending the program or the possible consequences of suspending it?		

Appendix D.4

War Through the Generations
Middle School English Language Arts

Directions: Choose the following three people: (a) a grandparent, (b) a parent, and (c) a peer. (If one of those people isn't available, you may choose someone else of a similar age.) Record their names at the top of this table. Then interview each person, using the two provided questions as well as additional questions we will create in class. Record each answer and be prepared to discuss your results back in our classroom.

	Name:	Name:	Name:
What memories of war do you have?			
How has war personally affected you?			

Appendix D.5

The Media's Impact on Physical Health
Middle School Physical Education

Directions: Survey 20 of your peers and record their answers below. One question is already given; as a class, we will design the remaining questions.

Question: Do you feel pressure from the media to maintain a certain weight?
Yes
Sometimes
No

Question:
Yes
Sometimes
No

Question:
Yes
Sometimes
No

Question:
Yes
Sometimes
No

Appendix E

High School Data Collection Tools

A data collection tool is aligned with each of the grade-level examples. They are labeled within each example and presented in the order they appear in the text.

DATA COLLECTION TOOLS

E.1: *Weighing Rights and Responsibilities,* High School Social Studies

E.2: *Environmental Application of Activation Energy,* High School Science

E.3: *The Function of Functions,* High School Mathematics

E.4: *Characters Wanted!* High School English Language Arts

E.5: *What Is in a Word?* High School Foreign Language

Appendix E.1

Weighing Rights and Responsibilities
High School Social Studies

Name _____   Date _____

Directions: Read and record responses to each of the following questions.

Student Response   **Parental Response**

1. Have you ever been a victim of discrimination? If yes, please explain the circumstances. Have you ever discriminated against someone based on age, race, gender, or political affiliation? Please explain.

2. In your opinion, is racism a natural human tendency, or is it a learned behavior? Explain.

3. In what ways does discrimination continue to exist today? Explain.

4. In your opinion, is it possible for people to overcome their differences and ultimately move beyond racism?

5. What factors hinder the healing of injustices? What factors encourage the healing of injustices?

6. In your opinion, what privileges are associated with being "white"? How are the colors "white" and "black" perceived differently throughout society?

Appendix E.2

Environmental Application of Activation Energy
High School Science

Name _____   Date _____

Directions: Identify at least three different areas or items in your home in which the concept of activation energy is important. Gather the following information for each item located.

Area/Item #1	Location in the Home	Description of Reaction	Level of Energy Required

Area/Item #2	Location in the Home	Description of Reaction	Level of Energy Required

Area/Item #3	Location in the Home	Description of Reaction	Level of Energy Required

Appendix E.3

The Function of Functions
High School Mathematics

Name _____   Date _____

Directions: Identify at least three different occupations in your community that utilize algebraic functions.

Occupational Area #1	Types of Functions Used	Examples of Functions

Occupational Area #2	Types of Functions Used	Examples of Functions

Occupational Area #3	Types of Functions Used	Examples of Functions

Appendix E.4

Characters Wanted!
High School English Language Arts

Name _____   Date _____

Directions: Use the following data collection tool as a preliminary template for building your resume. Feel free to use the template, but remember the resume *must* not exceed two pages (including references).

_____

Name:

Address:

Phone (If applicable):

Objectives:

Summary of Achievements:

Experience:

Education:

References (four needed):

Appendix E.5

What Is in a Word?
High School Foreign Language

Name _____   Date _____

Directions: Use this data collection template as a starting point for the one-page paper you will write.

What similarity between the languages will you explore? Why has this particular similarity been selected?

Speculate about the origins of such similarities.

Brainstorm places to research the origins of such a similarity.

Draft the opening paragraph of your paper.

A Guide to Your Professional Learning

Introduction

This guide offers an array of tools to assist you in processing the information found in Chapters 1–11, whether you are reading this book on your own; engaging in a grade-level, schoolwide, or districtwide professional development learning community; or using it in a college class.

There are multiple ways to process this information (i.e., speaking, listening, writing, mapping, drawing, charting, graphing, etc.). There are also many challenges involved in attempting to incorporate new practices into existing ones or replace habits that are not effective. Our hope is that getting to know the authors through the reading will lead you to examine your practice in order to find connections and disconnections with the text. Using the tools in this guide (and modifying them to fit your needs) should make it easier for you to self-audit, make changes, share your struggles and successes, and document your growth.

CO-CONSTRUCTED PORTFOLIO/JOURNAL

We hope that as the result of reading *Homework Done Right*, you will develop a deepened understanding and appreciation for the power of meaningful homework and will personally commit to enhancing your practice associated with this link in the learning cycle. It is our intent that you will become cognitively and emotionally connected to the content, carefully examine where you are in your development, and chart a course for expanding your practice using the principles and insights shared in this text.

Table A.1 Outline for Summarizing Results of Portfolio/Journal Assessments of My Own Teaching

	My Prereading Perspective	What I Learned	My Current Thoughts/Practices	My Plans for the Future
Chapter 1. What is so important about homework?				
Chapter 2. What is the rationale for homework?				
Chapter 3. What do the experts say about homework?				
Chapter 4. How does changing homework impact your practice?				
Chapter 5. How can you design meaningful homework?				
Chapter 6. How can you put meaningful homework into action?				
Chapters 7–10. Homework and the _____ Learner (Fill in the blank as appropriate.)				
Chapter 11. Still not convinced?				

1

What Is So Important About Homework?

REFLECTIVE QUESTIONS

1. What was the number one "Aha!" for you in Chapter 1? Why? How will you respond to it?

2. Do you agree that homework is a frequently underdeveloped link in the learning cycle? Why or why not?

3. How would your school board respond to the message conveyed in Chapter 1 that homework has untapped potential but also presents challenges. Why? (Consider asking school board members to read Chapter 1 and have a conversation with you about their reactions.)

ACTIVITIES FOR PROFESSIONAL LEARNING COMMUNITIES, FACULTY MEETINGS, AND OTHER GROUP INITIATIVES

1. As a group or in subgroups, ask the question "What do we believe about homework?" Record participant responses. Look for patterns. As a group, attempt to build some consensus. (Realize that you will not get agreement on everything, so begin by looking for agreements only!) Consider having the goal of writing a set of belief statements that the faculty would be willing to post and act upon. Revisit this statement and your actions periodically as you read the book. Discuss changes you would consider making to your initial statement. Make the changes when consensus is reached.

2. As a faculty, use the belief statements about homework to develop a plan to show what those beliefs would look like in action. Then determine the resources needed to enact your agreed-upon beliefs.

3. Examine the authors' beliefs expressed in Chapter 1 in light of those identified by your faculty. Draft a letter to families expressing what changes you are ready to consider regarding homework policies, why you are considering them, and how those changes would be revealed in students' out-of-school learning activities. Please note that dramatic changes probably will not occur initially. Revisit the letter draft as you read and discuss the ideas presented in the text. Revise the letter and send it when you feel comfortable about making some noticeable shifts in your approach to homework.

CHALLENGE YOURSELF

1. Identify the one belief expressed by the authors that resonates with you. Analyze last month's homework assignments to determine if your actions match that belief. If not, think about what you need to change as you enact upcoming homework. Commit to doing it!

2. Survey your classes by asking students to respond to the following question: What comes to mind when you hear the word *homework*? Hold a class discussion focusing on their answers.

3. Revisit the things that made you say, "That's me!" Select one that you want to abolish. Begin developing an action plan for making preliminary changes. Revisit the issue throughout your use of this book as you rethink homework.

2

What Is the Rationale for Homework?

REFLECTIVE QUESTIONS

1. Which of the principles of meaningful homework do you already enact? What evidence do you have that you are successful at doing this? What might you do to ensure an even higher success rate?

2. Which of the principles of meaningful homework identified by the authors do you think will be the most difficult for you to enact? Why? What might you do to capitalize on it?

3. Taking advantage of students' diversity by using it as a learning resource may touch on some sensitivities. What specifically will you do as you plan these homework learning opportunities to make sure diversity truly feels valued?

ACTIVITIES FOR PROFESSIONAL LEARNING COMMUNITIES, FACULTY MEETINGS, AND OTHER GROUP INITIATIVES

1. In faculty subgroups (designated by grade level or subject area), brainstorm possible ways that you might incorporate each principle of meaningful homework into your yearly planning. This list will grow as the year unfolds. For example, in a unit on community, you can expand meaningfulness and life application by encouraging students to study their environment. This could include encouraging them to gather photos, maps, and artifacts that represent their own community; talk to people in the community about how it has changed over time; take walking trips to unfamiliar local sites; etc.

2. Select the principle of meaningful home assignments that appears most difficult given your school community. Spend time discussing what you can do to overcome the challenge. Then select a topic that is addressed in more than one grade level and brainstorm meaningful homework possibilities.

3. Designate a meeting for discussing meaningful homework—specifically, the issue associated with teacher and family involvement. The introduction might go something like this:

For many, adult involvement in homework is a paradigm shift. What is your reaction to this? Why? What challenges does this present? How might we rethink this practice in our school? If we believe this is important, how should we approach it with our families and their children? What are the best ways to begin educating them about this shift? What sorts of responses can we anticipate? How will we address them?

CHALLENGE YOURSELF

1. Identify a principle of meaningful homework that you are somewhat comfortable addressing. Plan and implement in your next unit at least two goal-oriented home assignments that align with the principle you identify. Monitor students' responses to the assignments and plan adjustments accordingly.

2. Survey your class by asking students to respond to the following question: What is your reaction to having your family involved in your homework? Hold a class discussion focusing on their answers.

3. Select a home assignment that you know is tedious but that you cannot give up. Rote memorization exercises like memorizing multiplication tables, names of continents, rivers, natural resources of specified places, historical dates, famous speeches, or governmental processes are good candidates. Redesign your assignment so that it maintains the integrity of your original goal but adds at least two of the principles of meaningful homework described in this chapter.

3

What Do the Experts Say About Homework?

REFLECTIVE QUESTIONS

1. What was the most surprising thing you learned about homework as a result of reading this chapter?

2. What is your reaction to our proposed linking of homework and authentic learning? Explain.

3. What surprises you most about the history of homework? Think about your views within a historical perspective. For example, were you a student at the time of Sputnik and the subsequent shift in emphasis on homework? How has your history shaped your practice?

ACTIVITIES FOR PROFESSIONAL LEARNING COMMUNITIES, FACULTY MEETINGS, AND OTHER GROUP INITIATIVES

1. Ask the members of your group to read Chapter 3 prior to your meeting and to come prepared to take a position for or against homework. Consider assigning people debating roles opposite to their actual beliefs. After carefully examining both sides of the issue, conduct a second round of debates associated with whether or not homework should be authentic.

2. Discuss the school's policy associated with homework. What are the underlying assumptions? Based on the literature reviewed, is the policy viable? Why or why not? Should the policy be modified? If so, how?

3. Create a simple timeline that illustrates the six major shifts in how homework has been viewed. Each faculty member and the principal should independently plot where he or she fits on the timeline. Then conduct a large group discussion focusing on the patterns that emerge. Discuss possible reasons for your individual homework practices and how you have been influenced by your historical context. How do the principal's experiences weigh into his or her views and the school policy he or she supports? How do the school board members' or parents' histories weigh into their beliefs?

Our analysis divides the history of homework into five phases. This breakdown is not meant to be exhaustive but rather to provide an initial historical foundation for understanding where we are now in relation to the major homework reform movements of the past. While these phases are sequenced chronologically, we hesitate to apply a rigid set of dates because in some cases, the dates either were not explicit or were overlapping.

Where do you fit in? Where were you when? How has your own education influenced how you think about your practice?

Table A.2   History of Homework

	Robber Barons and Rote Memorization —> 1920s	The Rise of Progressive Education 1920s	Sputnik and the Age of Excellence 1950s	Risk and Renewed Age of Excellence 1980s	In Search of a Balanced Debate 2000s
Historical Catalyst	Minimal number of students enter high school; thus, homework is a nonissue for the majority of students.	The school becomes the optimal learning environment, and the teacher becomes the teaching expert.	Influential events include the launching of Sputnik, the Space Race and the rise of the Soviet "threat."	The release of *A Nation at Risk* and the rise of international economic competition influence thinking about education.	Homework receives increased media attention and becomes a renewed topic of debate among educators.
Pedagogy/ Curriculum	Drill, memorization and recitation	Learner-centered	Emphasis on rigor, especially as it relates to math and science	Back-to-basics emphasis with renewed attention given to math and science	Narrowing of curriculum due to standards and testing
Views of Homework	Favorable	Unfavorable	Favorable	Favorable	Mixed

CHALLENGE YOURSELF

1. The literature presented leans toward the use of authentic tasks in an effort to foster curiosity and enhance meaningfulness. Collect and analyze the homework that you assigned during your last unit in one of the subjects you teach. How would you rate yourself? Why? If you have an unsatisfactory rating, think about what you need to change and why. Commit to making the necessary changes in your next unit.

2. Conduct a mini action research project in your classroom in an effort to determine what happens when you change the nature of homework. Study student responses over several weeks to determine how they respond when you make the tasks more authentic. What happens when they engage their families in the authentic tasks that you assign?

3. A common thread among those who oppose homework is the claim that it widens the gap between privileged and disadvantaged students. Study this claim in terms of your class. Is it true? If so, design a plan that offsets this problem. Make accommodations so that all students will be interested in the tasks and will be successful.

4

How Does Changing Homework Impact Your Practice?

REFLECTIVE QUESTIONS

1. Which of the teacher stories do I identify with most closely? Why?

2. What evidence do I have that I need to rethink some of my homework practices?

3. How are the families of my students responding to the current homework assignments?

ACTIVITIES FOR PROFESSIONAL LEARNING COMMUNITIES, FACULTY MEETINGS, AND OTHER GROUP INITIATIVES

1. Assign one vignette as prework to each of four faculty groups. During the faculty small-group time, create a profile of the teacher and discuss the highlights of his or her story. What is most compelling regarding what happened in that teacher's classroom? Why?

2. As a faculty, unpack the key components of each of the teacher stories. Discuss how their struggles are similar or dissimilar to the ones you face in your school. What additional struggles do you face that were not mentioned in their stories?

3. Brainstorm the homework challenges you face as a faculty. Then, using the Problem-Solving Strategy (see below), decide on your top priority and work toward a solution as a group:

Designate three people to participate. All others are "balcony people" who simply listen.

Assign a recorder to document all responses.

Each step is timed. The group decides in advance how much time to allocate for each component.[1]

Problem-Solving Strategy

1. Identify the problem. Describe every detail. Designate one spokesperson.

2. Pose questions about the problem.

3. Brainstorm all possible solutions. Spokesperson does not talk; the other two people brainstorm.

4. Spokesperson selects one item from brainstormed list to talk about and propose to work on as the priority.

CHALLENGE YOURSELF

1. Craft your own "teacher story" regarding homework in your classroom. Select a colleague and discuss it. What patterns emerged? What did you learn about yourself and your practice? What would you like to change/modify? How might you begin to make the shift?

2. Select one of the teachers' stories from the text that resonates closely with yours. Generate a list of questions you would ask that teacher. Then recruit a colleague who is familiar with that teacher's story to talk about your questions. Speculate how Barbara, Rob, Sarah, or Ben would respond. Generate next steps for you to take in order to begin shifting your homework paradigm.

3. Revisit the teachers' stories and identify one or two changes the teachers made that you could make immediately. Enact the change(s) and note what happens for you and your students.

---

[1]Modification for large group: There is no limit to the number of individuals who can be active participants. Designated time (identified in advance) is key.

5

How Can You Design Meaningful Homework?

REFLECTIVE QUESTIONS

1. What evidence do I have that my homework assignments align with the primary principles for selecting activities in all school subjects (i.e., goal relevance, appropriate level of difficulty, feasibility, and cost)? What modifications do I need to make?

2. What evidence do I have that my home assignments serve more than one goal when possible? Provide motivational value? Incorporate higher-order thinking? Include variety? Use assets? Incorporate student voice? How can I prioritize the modifications I still need to make?

3. In designing my homework activities, what evidence do I have that I give adequate thought to the forms needed for students to use in retrieving information? What sorts of enhancements do I need to make? What evidence do I have that I give adequate attention to how the homework assignments will be used back in the classroom? What adjustments do I need to make?

ACTIVITIES FOR PROFESSIONAL LEARNING COMMUNITIES, FACULTY MEETINGS, AND OTHER GROUP INITIATIVES

1. Bring a recent homework assignment to the next staff meeting to be critiqued in light of the factors described in this chapter. What aspects of your assignment are validated? What needs more of your attention? How will you proceed?

2. Encourage every faculty member to bring examples of homework assignments that have been implemented in the classroom and to bring back the results. Analyze the examples in terms of the principles applied. Were some

principles emphasized more than others? Discuss the challenges that still need to be addressed.

3. Focus a faculty meeting on the topic of "Standards Come to Life." Encourage faculty members to volunteer to serve on a panel to discuss the power of meaningful homework in bringing the standards to life. Panel members should be encouraged to bring concrete examples to illustrate their responses. Allow time for Q & A.

4. Consider allocating a faculty meeting to discussing local community, school, and student assets and how these can be made more transparent and leveraged for future homework opportunities.

CHALLENGE YOURSELF

1. Using what you have learned in this chapter regarding meaningful homework design, create an assignment for an upcoming unit that you would submit as award winning. Implement it!

2. Partner with one or more teachers of other school subject areas to design and use a meaningful cross-curricular home assignment that meets several (if not all) of the principles described in this chapter.

3. Audiotape lessons that call for bringing the homework responses back to the classroom to be integral parts of in-class sessions. Listen for the use of inquiry skills. Which skills were emphasized? Which skills could naturally be added? Which skills need more attention as evidenced by students' responses?

4. Audiotape class sessions where home assignments are "harvested." What evidence is there that the students draw heavily on their assets? What are their responses to this practice?

6

How Can You Put Meaningful Homework Into Action?

REFLECTIVE QUESTIONS

1. What were the two most powerful insights you acquired as the result of reading this chapter? How will you incorporate them into your practice?

2. What is one idea put forth in this chapter that you think might be impossible to implement in your classroom? Share the idea with three colleagues and elicit their ideas and opinions. Find a colleague who will help you shift your thinking.

3. Modeling is an important component in ensuring the success of meaningful homework. Monitor this practice over the next several weeks. With what facet of it are you most successful? Least successful? Commit yourself to making the needed modifications.

ACTIVITIES FOR PROFESSIONAL LEARNING COMMUNITIES, FACULTY MEETINGS, AND OTHER GROUP INITIATIVES

1. Group faculty members by grade level or content areas. Have each group prepare a "mind movie" (drawings/words) of how it will put homework into action. Look for patterns across the "movies" for elements that will be emphasized. Critique each other's "movies" for key elements that have been forgotten.

2. Have faculty members work in triads. From the chapter, select the two most difficult/challenging elements of putting meaningful homework into action.

Discuss why they are difficult and specifically what you would do to overcome the barriers. Share results with the large group.

3. Reflect on the example homework assignment that focuses on unions. As a faculty, discuss what made this such a powerful homework assignment. What insights did you acquire from reading this example? What questions do you still have? How do you think your students would respond to this assignment? Why? How would your students' families respond? Why?

CHALLENGE YOURSELF

1. Study the home assignments you have given over the last several weeks. Which were most successful? Why? Least successful? Why? Use this chapter to determine which of the key points you need to think more about. To which of the points do you need to pay more attention as you move ahead with your homework agenda?

2. Study home assignment returns from your students. When do you have the lowest return rate? Highest return rate? Is the return rate higher or lower among females, males, special needs students, or some other group? Use these data to drive your future decisions associated with home assignments.

3. Design a class survey to determine how students feel about the changes in their homework assignments. After analyzing the data, hold a class discussion. Clear up misconceptions and reiterate the value of authentic assignments.

7–10

How Can Meaningful Homework Look?

REFLECTIVE QUESTIONS

1. How can I design more homework assignments that use the strengths of my students?

2. How can I pay more attention to the particular needs of my students as described by the authors?

3. What can I do to make my homework assignments more appropriate and sensitive to the needs of my students?

4. What holds me back from designing more homework assignments that are more meaningful?

ACTIVITIES FOR PROFESSIONAL LEARNING COMMUNITIES, FACULTY MEETINGS, AND OTHER GROUP INITIATIVES

1. Bring a recent homework assignment to the next staff meeting to be critiqued in light of what we have been learning in this book.

2. Interview students, parents, or community members before the next faculty meeting to elicit their thoughts about homework. Share the results with your colleagues.

3. Together with your colleagues, identify the next steps you need to take to make more of your homework assignments more meaningful. Ask: How can we support each other to ensure that we sustain the momentum?

4. Revisit the parent letter you drafted earlier. Have you sent it? Does it need revision? Consider writing an initial follow-up letter to parents describing the changes in culture that your building is attempting to make in light of reading this book.

5. Write and submit an article to the school or local newspaper describing homework done right in your school district.

CHALLENGE YOURSELF

1. Using what you have learned in discussing homework with students, parents, and community members and at recent faculty meetings, design a proposal for an upcoming conference so you can share your ideas with peers at other locations.

2. Partner with one or more teachers of other subject areas to design and use a meaningful cross-curricular homework assignment.

3. Informally interview students and/or family members after implementing several authentic home assignments to determine their overall reactions to the shift. Be prepared to make any needed adjustments. The goal is to make sure the changes are understood, communicated, and make sense given your unique teaching situation.

11

Still Not Convinced?

REFLECTIVE QUESTIONS

1. After reading this chapter, with which of the challenges are you more at ease? Why? Specifically, how will you initially address them?

2. Which of the challenges had you not previously considered? How will addressing them influence your practice?

3. Are you still uncomfortable with any of the challenges? Why? Where might you go for advice?

ACTIVITIES FOR PROFESSIONAL LEARNING COMMUNITIES, FACULTY MEETINGS, AND OTHER GROUP INITIATIVES

1. Prior to a work session, group faculty members by grade level or content area. Have each group member identify one challenge from each category that he or she would like to discuss. When the groups convene, they will discuss the identified challenges so each member will feel more comfortable with the challenge he or she views as most critical to realizing success with homework.

2. Appoint someone to provide a brief overview of your school's policy associated with homework. Then, in triads, have faculty members review and discuss the school culture challenges. After adequate small-group time, share the responses with the whole group. Design a plan for addressing these challenges at the school level.

3. One of the administrator challenges relates to staff development for helping teachers be more successful with meaningful homework. As a faculty, design

a plan for addressing this issue. If you are already making lots of changes in your homework, what sorts of support would help you sustain the momentum? Create an agenda for the first one to two sessions.

CHALLENGE YOURSELF

1. Select a student subgroup (e.g., special needs students, gifted students, ELL students) and monitor their responses to your more authentic homework practices. What patterns emerge? What modifications seem to be most successful? Least successful? What future changes do you plan on making?

2. Monitor the homework from students who split time between two households. What patterns emerge? Which of your strategic moves yield the most positive results? Which seem to have no impact? What future changes will you consider making?

3. Consider the administrator challenge associated with supporting teachers who strive to "push the envelope" in their use of homework as a learning tool. What advice would you give to the building leader? Write it down and set an appointment to share your ideas and insights.

Index

Accountability, 63–64
Achebe, C., 112
Action plans
  communication strategies, 58–59
  evaluation strategies, 62–63
  family involvement, 61
  home visits, 61–62
  instructional uses of assignments, 62
  modeling strategies, 60
  organizational tools, 60
  participation rates, 61
  showcasing and celebrating student work, 63
Activation energy assignment, 107–109, 171–172
Adaptability, 44
Administrator challenges, 123
Adult involvement, 10, 120
Alleman, J., 5, 9, 12, 21, 28, 42, 43
Amanti, C., 44
Ancestry assignment, 70–71, 142
Anticipated barriers, 57
Anti-homework proponents, 18–21
Appropriate level of difficulty, 43
Art assignments, 90–92, 159
Artistic visionaries assignment, 90–92, 159
Assessment strategies, 64–65
Assets, 44–45, 56, 120, 130
Assignment buddies, 60, 61
Assignment descriptions, 55
Assignment extensions, 57, 62, 131
Assignment goals, 55, 62
Assignment timeline, 55–56, 61, 64
Authentic learning, 4, 15, 21–24, 62
  see also Meaningful homework
Auto industry assignment, 128–140

Barriers, 57, 131
Basic principles
  diverse perspectives, 11–12
  expanding meaningfulness, 9
  life applications, 8–9
  natural opportunities, 9
  out-of-school cost-effective opportunities, 12–13
  parental involvement, 10
  personalized curriculum, 12
  up-to-date resources, 13

Basic skills practice, 5
Beane, J., 91
Bigelow, B., 130
Botwinski, Ben, 35–39
Brainstorming, 60, 122
Brophy, J., 5, 9, 12, 21, 28, 42, 43
Buddies, 60, 61
Buell, J., 18, 19, 20, 34
Buy-in, 60

Carbon footprint assignment, 96–98, 163
Center for Authentic Task Design, 23
Clothing Museum assignment, 74–75, 144–145
Collaborative learning, 10
College-bound students, 118–119
Collier, C., 101
Collier, J., 101
Communication strategies
  completed design planning form, 130
  expectations, 63–64
  family involvement, 56, 58–59, 61
Community assets, 44–45, 56, 130
Conferences, 61
Cooper, H., 16, 17, 19, 21, 34
  see also Muhlenbruck, L.
Cost-effectiveness, 43
Cost-effective opportunities, 12–13
Course grades, 18–19
Creemers, B. P. M., 17
Cross talk questions
  art assignment, 92
  English/language arts assignment, 79, 88, 101–102, 112–113
  foreign languages, 114
  mathematics assignment, 77, 90, 95–96, 110–111
  physical education assignment, 103
  science assignment, 73, 85–86, 97–98, 108–109
  social studies assignment, 71, 75, 83–84, 99–100, 107

Data collection and analysis
  early elementary grades, 141–147
  high school, 167–180
  inquiry skills, 47–48
  middle school grades, 161–166
  upper elementary grades, 149–159

Deadlines, 60, 61, 64
de Jong, R., 17
Design guidelines
    design factors, 42–45
    design planning form, 51–57, 128–140
    inquiry skills, 45–51
Design planning form
    completed form example, 128–140
    homework design planning form, 51–54
    usage strategies, 54–57
Difficulty levels, 43
Disadvantaged students, 19, 33–34
Disposable cameras, 94–96
District-level policies and practices, 123
Diverse perspectives, 11–12
Doyle, W., 8

Early elementary grades
    data collection tools, 141–147
    English/language arts assignment, 77–79, 147
    instructional strategies, 69–70
    mathematics assignment, 76–77, 146
    meaningful homework, 69–79
    response strategies, 26–29
    science assignment, 72–73, 143
    social studies assignment, 70–71, 74–75,
        142, 144–145
Economics assignment, 128–140
Editorial writing assignment, 86–88, 155–156
Effective writing assignment, 111–113, 175–176
English/language arts assignments
    early elementary grades, 77–79, 147
    high school, 111–113, 175–176
    middle school grades, 100–102, 165
    upper elementary grades, 86–88, 155–156
English language learners (ELLs), 117–118
Evaluation strategies, 62–63
Evidence collecion, 48–49
Expectations, 63–64
Extrinsic motivation, 119

Faculty meeting activities, 184–200
Family assets, 44–45, 56, 130
Family challenges, 119–121
Family involvement
    auto industry assignment, 128–140
    grading policies, 122
    home visits, 61–62
    homework assignments, 14, 35–39, 56, 58–59, 61
    lower elementary grades, 26–29
Feasibility, 43
Feedback, 60, 61, 62
Fine arts program assignments, 98–100, 164
Foreign language assignments, 113–114, 177–178
Fried, R., 21, 22
Function of functions assignment, 109–111,
    173–174
Funds of knowledge, 44–45

Gamoran, A., 24
Gentry, M., 22, 23
Gifted and talented learners, 117
Glasser, W., 28
Goal relevance, 43, 122
Gonzalez, N., 44
Good, T., 21
Grades, 62–63, 119, 122
Graphic organizers, 60
Group activities, 184–200

Hesse, H., 112
Higher order thinking skills, 44
High school
    data collection tools, 167–180
    English/language arts assignment, 111–113,
        175–176
    foreign languages, 113–114, 177–178
    mathematics assignment, 109–111, 173–174
    meaningful homework, 104–115
    response strategies, 35–39
    science assignment, 107–109, 171–172
    social studies assignment, 105–107, 168–172
Home visits, 61–62
Homework
    background information, 15–16
    continuum approach, 5–6
    frustrations, 2–3
    guidelines, 21
    negative effects, 18–21
    positive effects, 16–18
    rationale, 8–14
    "We Believe" statements, 4–5
    see also Meaningful homework

Informative writing assignment, 175–176
Inquiry process
    data collection and analysis, 47–48
    evidence collecion, 48–49
    homework design planning form, 55
    importance, 45–46
    instructional strategies, 50–51
    observation skills, 48
    problem identification skills, 46–47
    questioning skills, 46
    reflection and summarization activities, 49–50
    source selection and evaluation, 48–49
    workshop lesson steps, 51
Instructional uses of assignments, 56–57, 62
Integration opportunities, 57, 62
Intrinsic motivation, 119

Journal assessment guidelines, 182–183

Kastens, C., 17
Knapp, M. S., 24
Knighton, Barbara, 26–29
Kohn, A., 5, 18–19, 20, 28, 34

Koller, O., 17
Kralovec, E., 18, 19, 20, 34

Language comparison assignment, 113–114,
    177–178
Learning disabled students, 116–117
Level of difficulty, 43
Levy, S., 30, 32
Ley, Rob, 29–32
Life applications, 8–12
Lindsay, J. J.
    see Muhlenbruck, L.
Ludtke, O., 17

Marks, H., 24
Marzano, R. J., 16, 17, 18, 21, 34
Mathematics assignments
    early elementary grades, 76–77, 146
    high school, 109–111, 173–174
    middle school grades, 94–96, 162
    upper elementary grades, 88–90, 157–158
Math pairs assignment, 76–77, 146
Meaningful homework
    action plans, 58–63
    administrator challenges, 123
    assessment strategies, 64–65
    basic principles, 8–13
    characteristics, 3–4
    continuum approach, 5–6
    design guidelines, 42–57
    early elementary grades, 69–79
    expectations, 63–64
    family challenges, 119–121
    high school, 104–115
    illustrative examples, 67–68
    instructional strategies, 6–7
    middle school grades, 93–94
    participation rates, 63–64
    professional learning guide, 181–200
    reflective questions and activities, 184–200
    response strategies, 26–39
    school culture challenges, 123–124
    student challenges, 116–119
    teacher challenges, 121–122
    teacher involvement, 13–14
    upper elementary grades, 80–92
    "We Believe" statements, 4–5
    see also Design planning form; Family
        involvement
Media and physical health assignment,
    102–103, 166
Metric system assignment, 88–90, 157–158
Middle school
    data collection tools, 161–166
    English/language arts assignment,
        100–102, 165
    mathematics assignment, 94–96, 162
    meaningful homework, 93–94

physical education assignment, 102–103, 167
response strategies, 33–35
science assignment, 96–98, 163
social studies assignment, 98–100, 165
Middlestead, Sarah, 33–35
Moll, L., 44
Monitoring strategies, 61
Motivational value, 44, 60, 119
Muhlenbruck, L., 17
Multiple goals, 43–44

Neff, D., 44
Newmann, F., 4, 22–24, 34
Nye, B.
    see Muhlenbruck, L.

Observation skills, 48
Organizational tools, 56, 60, 130, 182–183
Out-of-date resources, 13
Out-of-school learning activities, 9–13

Pair-share, 60
Parental involvement, 10, 104–107, 122
Parent–child relationships, 19–20
Patall, E., 17, 21
Paterson, K., 131
Patterns to Algebra assignment, 94–96, 162
Personalized curriculum, 12
Persuasive writing assignment, 175–176
Photographic assignment, 94–96
Physical education assignments, 102–103, 166
Pickering, D. J., 16, 17, 18, 21
Pope, D. C., 2
Portfolios, 182–183
Problem identification skills, 46–47
Professional learning community activities, 184–200
Professional learning guide, 181–200

Questioning skills, 46

Rationale, 8–14
Real-life problem-solving, 23, 46–47, 122
Reflection and summarization activities, 49–50
Reis, S., 22, 23
Relevant standards, 55
Renzulli, J., 22, 23
Resume assignment, 175–176
Rights and responsibilities assignment, 105–107,
    168–172
Robinson, J., 17, 21
Role-play strategies, 60
Rubrics, 62–63
Rule, A., 21

School culture challenges, 123–124
Science assignments
    early elementary grades, 72–73, 143
    high school, 107–109, 171–172

middle school grades, 96–98, 163
upper elementary grades, 84–86, 154
Sedgwick, M., 101
Self-efficacy, 9
Self-regulation, 9
Showcasing and celebrating student work, 63
Situated learning, 9
Social-class inequities, 19
Social studies assignments
early elementary grades, 70–71, 74–75, 142, 144–145
high school, 105–107, 168–172
middle school grades, 98–100, 164
upper elementary grades, 81–84, 150–153
Socioeconomic status, 119–120
Source selection and evaluation, 48–49
Special needs students, 116–117
Staff development, 123
Standards of instruction, 4
Student achievement, 17–19
Student assets, 44–45, 56, 130
Student challenges, 116–119
Student voice and choice, 45, 56
Sueker, E., 20

Table talk, 60
Tan, A., 112
Teacher challenges, 121–122
Tension, 19–20
Timelines, 55–56, 61, 64
Time management strategies, 121–122
Time-sensitive resources, 13
Traditional homework, 124

Trautwein, U., 17
Traveling mascot assignment, 77–79, 147
Two-household environments, 120–121

Upper elementary grades
art assignment, 90–92, 159
data collection tools, 149–159
English/language arts assignment, 86–88, 155–156
homework importance, 80–81
mathematics assignment, 88–90, 157–158
meaningful homework, 80–92
response strategies, 29–32
science assignment, 84–86, 154
social studies assignment, 81–84, 150–153
standardized tests, 80–81
Up-to-date resources, 13

Voter registration assignment, 81–84, 150–153

Wallis, C., 19, 21
War through the generations assignment, 100–102, 165
Weather reporting assignment, 72–73, 143
"We Believe" statements, 4–5
Wehlage, G., 4
Westerhof, K. J., 17
Wheelchair accessibility rights assignment, 84–86, 154
Wiesel, E., 101

Zais, R., 42